Age 5-7 English

I Can Lear

Mega English

Contributions by Nicola Morgan and Lindsay Hancock
Cover and interior illustrations by John Haslam, Pip Adams and Craig Cameron

EGMONT
We bring stories to life

First published in Great Britain in 2005 by Egmont UK Limited
239 Kensington High Street, London W8 6SA
Published in this edition in 2011

ISBN 978 1 4052 5895 1
1 3 5 7 9 10 8 6 4 2
Printed in Italy

Contents

Contents

About this book

Mega English 5–7 offers lots of practice in English skills as described in the guidelines for the National Literacy Strategy. The book reflects the content of the National Curriculum in England and Wales and the 5–14 programme in Scotland.

The book is divided into three sections. The content of each section reflects what is taught from the National Literacy Strategy.

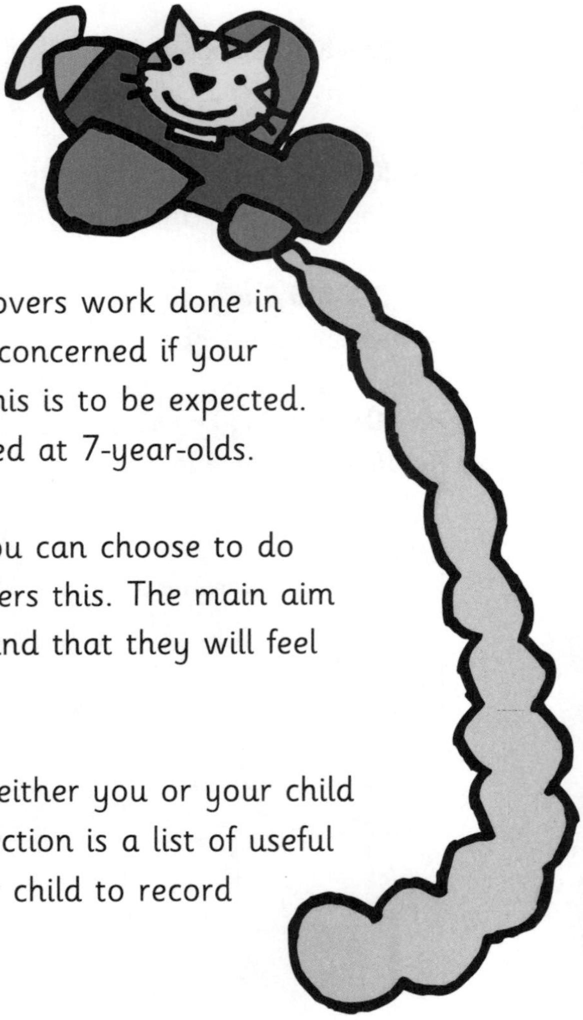

1. Reading Comprehension
2. Spelling Skills
3. Writing Composition

This book is aimed at children aged 5–7 years. It covers work done in school in Reception, Year 1 and Year 2, so don't be concerned if your 5-year-old needs help with many of the activities. This is to be expected. Some topics may seem ambitious but these are aimed at 7-year-olds.

Activities within each section are progressive, but you can choose to do a little at a time from each section if your child prefers this. The main aim is to start with something that interests your child and that they will feel confident about tackling.

Answers appear at the end of each section, so that either you or your child can check and mark the work. After each answer section is a list of useful words and a checklist, which will help you and your child to record progress made.

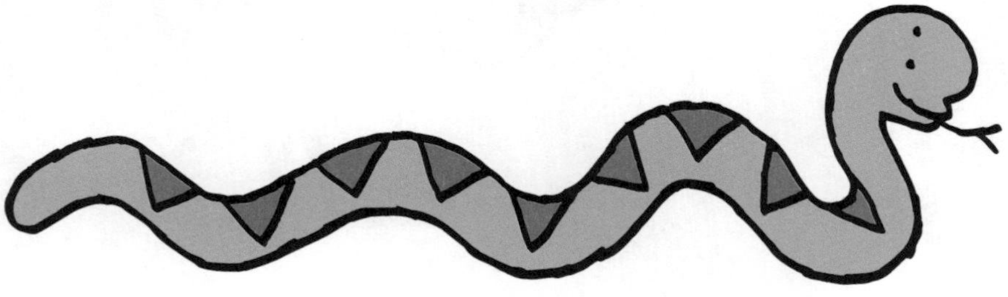

Finding your way around

Checklist to tick off your child's achievements.

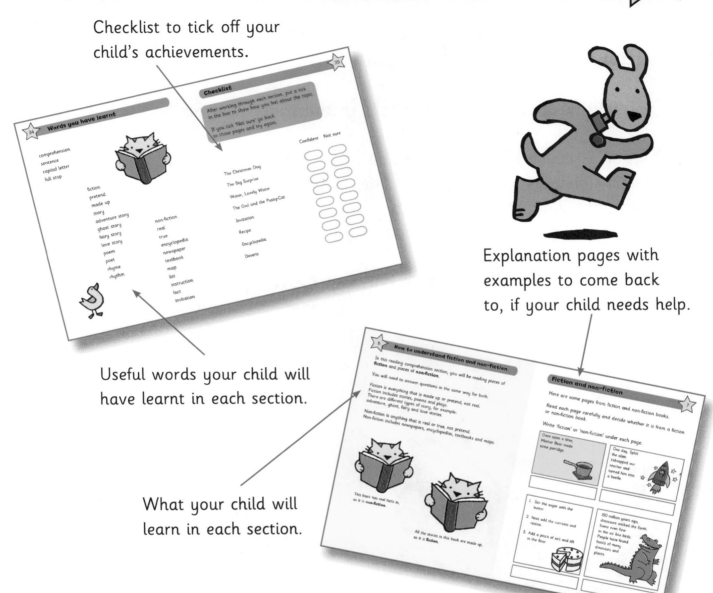

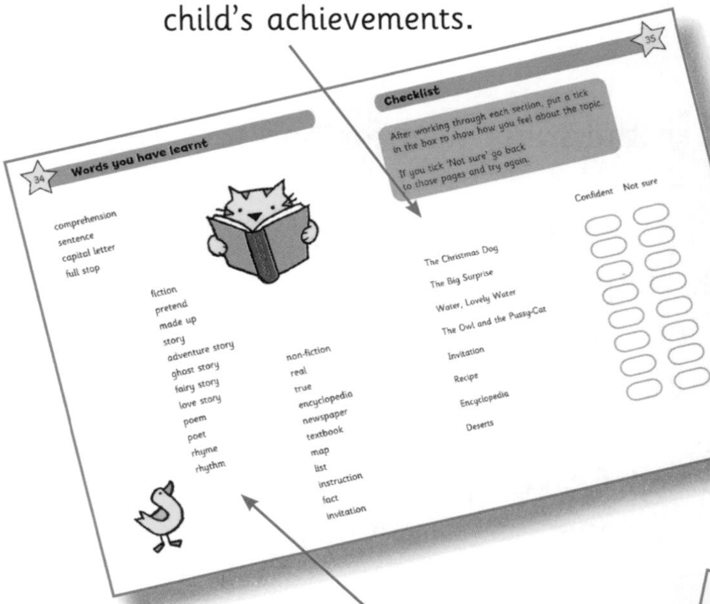

Explanation pages with examples to come back to, if your child needs help.

Useful words your child will have learnt in each section.

What your child will learn in each section.

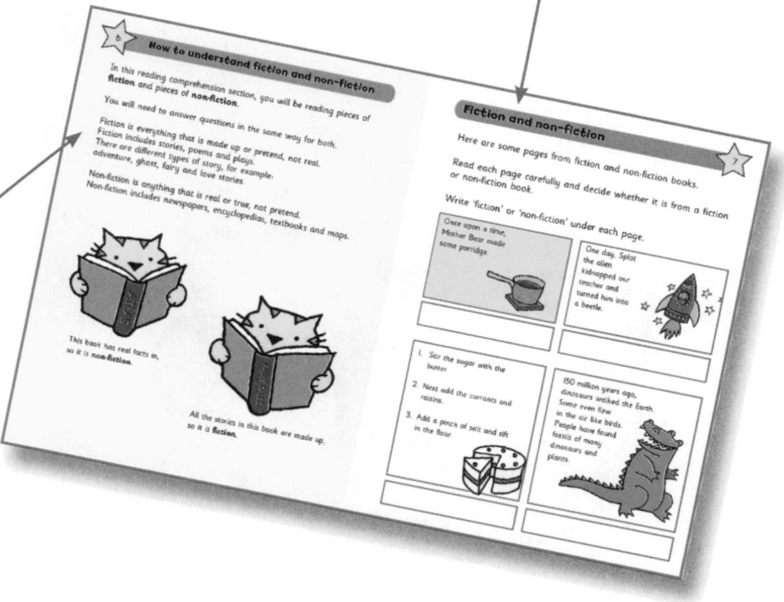

How to help your child

Let your child decide how long they want to work on the book.
The book is designed for your child to start and stop any time they wish.
Give lots of encouragement and praise for effort.

Instructions are written clearly and simply, but you will need to look through the activities and explain what your child is being asked to do. If your child has problems with a type of activity, talk about it together and try to help. You may need to discuss it with your child's class teacher.

How to understand fiction and non-fiction

In this reading comprehension section, you will be reading pieces of **fiction** and pieces of **non-fiction**.

You will need to answer questions in the same way for both.

Fiction is everything that is made up or pretend, not real.
Fiction includes stories, poems and plays.
There are different types of story, for example:
adventure, ghost, fairy and love stories.

Non-fiction is anything that is real or true, not pretend.
Non-fiction includes newspapers, encyclopedias, textbooks and maps.

This book has real facts in,
so it is **non-fiction**.

All the stories in this book are made up,
so it is **fiction**.

Fiction and non-fiction

Here are some pages from fiction and non-fiction books.

Read each page carefully and decide whether it is from a fiction or non-fiction book.

Write 'fiction' or 'non-fiction' under each page.

Once upon a time, Mother Bear made some porridge.

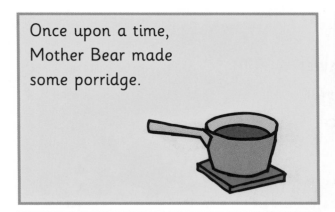

One day, Splot the alien kidnapped our teacher and turned him into a beetle.

1. Stir the sugar with the butter.
2. Next add the currants and raisins.
3. Add a pinch of salt and sift in the flour.

150 million years ago, dinosaurs walked the Earth. Some even flew in the air like birds. People have found fossils of many dinosaurs and plants.

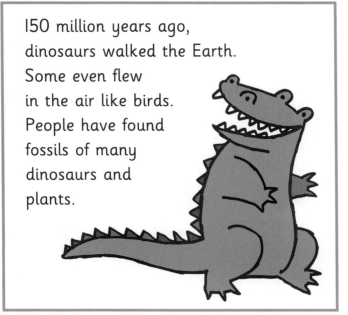

Reading comprehension - fiction

Reading comprehension is a way of checking that you have understood what you have been reading.
The following pages have many pieces of writing to read and questions to answer.

Read the piece of writing as many times as you like before you answer the questions.

There are two different ways to answer the questions:
1. Tick the box with the correct answer.
2. Answer the question in a sentence.

When answering the questions, you will be learning different reading comprehension skills:

How to look for facts.
How to understand why things happen.
How to understand what's going on.
How to look for words and understand what they mean.

Parent note:
With a 5-year-old or beginner reader you will need to read the passages and discuss the answers together.

Reading comprehension – fiction

Look at this example that has been filled in for you.

Billy's Big Match

Billy loved to play football. His favourite position was centre-forward. He loved scoring goals and hearing the crowd chant his name. Little was Billy to realise that the next game he would play would change his life forever ...

1. What does Billy love to do?

- [ ] **play rugby**
- [ ] **go to school**
- [ ] **eat chocolate**
- [x] **play football**

2. What position does Billy love to play?

- [ ] **goalie**
- [x] **centre-forward**
- [ ] **right back**
- [ ] **midfield**

3. Which word means to sing or shout? **chant**

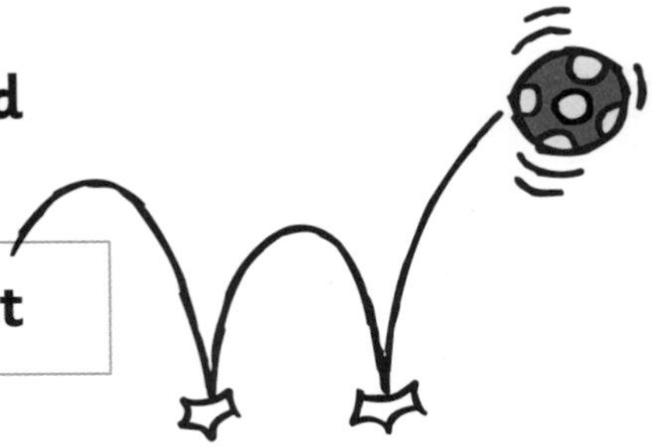

4. What will happen in the next game?

Billy's life will change forever.

Reading comprehension – fiction

The Christmas Dog

One week after Christmas, Sally and Ben found a little dog on the doorstep. He looked tired and cold and very hungry.

"You poor thing," said Dad. "Let's give you some food and water and get you warm."

"Can't we keep him?" asked Ben.

"No, he belongs to someone else," replied Dad. "His owner will be missing him."

1. When did the children find the dog?

☐ **on Christmas Day** ☐ **a week before Christmas**

☐ **on the doorstep** ☐ **a week after Christmas**

2. Who wanted to keep the dog?

☐ **Sally** ☐ **Ben**

☐ **Dad** ☐ **the dog**

3. Why did Dad say they could not keep the dog?

____

____

____

Reading comprehension – fiction

Sally and Ben gave the little dog food and made a cosy bed for him near the fire. They wished they could keep him. But that evening a man from a special dog home took the dog away. Sally and Ben were very sad.

A week later, Mum came home with a big box. In it was the little dog! "We can keep the dog because his owner doesn't want him any more," she said.

"Hooray!" shouted Sally and Ben in delight. "Let's call him 'Christmas'," said Sally.

4. Where did the children make a bed for the dog?

☐ **in a big box** ☐ **in a special dog home**

☐ **near the fire** ☐ **in the kitchen**

5. Why were they able to keep the dog?

☐ **because they wanted him** ☐ **because his owner didn't want him**

☐ **because it was Christmas** ☐ **because they were sad**

6. How did they feel when Mum said they could keep the dog?

____

7. Did you like the end of this story? Why?

____

____

Reading comprehension - fiction

The Big Surprise

Jack found some seeds in the garden shed. He planted one in some soil in a small pot. He put some water on the soil and left the pot in a sunny place. Each day he looked to see if anything was growing. Sometimes he put more water on the soil.

After ten days a small green leaf appeared. "Hooray!" said Jack. "I wonder what it is?"

1. Where did Jack find the seeds?

☐ **in the soil** ☐ **in a sunny place**

☐ **in the garden shed** ☐ **in the water**

2. How often did Jack water the soil?

☐ **every day** ☐ **never**

☐ **sometimes** ☐ **twice**

3. Why did Jack say "Hooray!" when he saw the leaf?

____

____

____

Reading comprehension – fiction

In the next week, the plant grew, and grew. Mum said it needed a bigger pot so she helped Jack to move it.

Soon the plant had ten leaves and was too big for its new pot. It was almost as tall as Jack.

"I still don't know what sort of plant it is," said Jack. "Do you know, Mum?"

Mum didn't say anything, she just smiled.

4. What did Mum and Jack do to the plant?

☐ **they made it bigger** ☐ **they put it in a bigger pot**

☐ **they put it in the garden** ☐ **they tied it to a stick**

5. Why did the plant need a bigger pot again?

____

____

6. How tall was the plant?

☐ **taller than Jack** ☐ **as tall as Mum**

☐ **nearly as tall as Jack** ☐ **ten metres tall**

7. On this page, did Mum tell Jack what the plant was?

____

Reading comprehension - fiction

The plant grew taller and taller. Mum planted it in the garden and Jack could see it from his bedroom window.

One night, Mum read Jack a bedtime story called Jack and the Beanstalk. In the story, the beanstalk grew as high as the clouds and there was an angry giant living at the top with lots of gold.

“Maybe my plant is a beanstalk!” shouted Jack. “Maybe I will find gold at the top of it!”

“Well, don’t try climbing it,” said Mum firmly. “You might fall.”

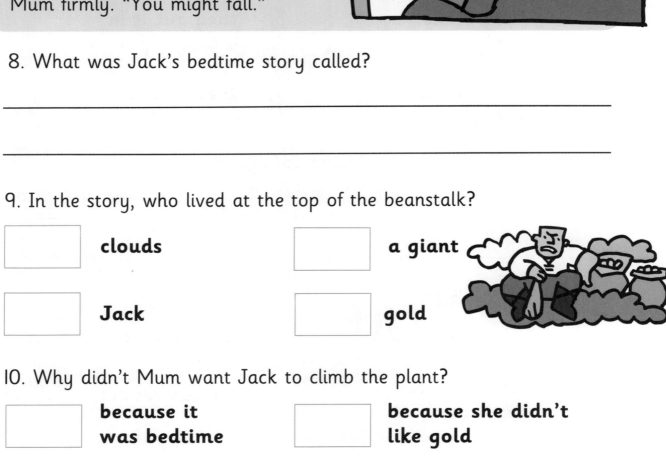

8. What was Jack’s bedtime story called?

____

____

9. In the story, who lived at the top of the beanstalk?

- [ ] **clouds**
- [ ] **a giant**
- [ ] **Jack**
- [ ] **gold**

10. Why didn’t Mum want Jack to climb the plant?

- [ ] **because it was bedtime**
- [ ] **because she didn’t like gold**
- [ ] **because he might fall**
- [ ] **because of the angry giant**

The next day Jack went outside to play.
When he saw his plant, his eyes opened wide in surprise.

"Mum, Mum, Mum. Come and look!" he yelled. Mum came running, thinking that something terrible had happened. She saw the plant. It had a huge yellow flower at the top, with a round brown middle.

"It's a sunflower!" she said. "And it's taller than me. We must enter it for the flower show – it might win a prize."

Jack looked after his plant very well. And, guess what? He did win first prize at the show, which was much better than an angry giant and lots of gold.

11. What colour was the middle of the flower?

- [ ] **yellow**
- [ ] **green**
- [ ] **brown**

12. Why did Mum think something terrible had happened?

____

____

13. Where did Jack win a prize for his sunflower?

- [ ] **because it was tall**
- [ ] **in the garden**
- [ ] **at the flower show**
- [ ] **in a pot**

Water, Lovely Water

Many hundreds of miles away in Africa, a girl called Salma lived with her family. Everyone in Salma's village helped to work on the land. They grew fruit and vegetables and kept animals too.

They grew their own food, but if there was any spare food they would sell it at the market. With the money this made they could buy the things which they couldn't grow, like clothes, soap, oil and tools. They kept cows and goats, which they could sell as well. The cows and goats gave them milk.

Everyone had to work hard. But the worst thing was that they had no water in the village. Every day, all the women had to carry heavy jars of water from the river.
The water was dirty and sometimes made people ill. The women did not complain. They had been doing it for years, and they needed the water for themselves, their animals and to grow their food.

1. How far away is Africa?

☐ **nearby**

☐ **hundreds of miles away**

☐ **thousands of miles away**

☐ **far away**

2. Where did the people go to sell things?

☐ **the village** ☐ **the market**

☐ **a farm** ☐ **a shop**

3. Write three things the story says people needed but couldn't grow.

☐ ☐ ☐

4. Who had to work hard?

☐ **Salma** ☐ **animals**

☐ **everyone** ☐ **they didn't work hard**

5. What was the biggest problem the villagers had?

☐

6. Who fetched water every day?

☐ **Salma** ☐ **everyone**

☐ **the children** ☐ **all the women**

7. There were two reasons why the women did not complain.
Tick the two that you learn from the story.

☐ **they had been doing it for years** ☐ **they had nothing else to do**

☐ **water helped their food to grow**

Then one day, some strangers arrived in the village with a lot of trucks and diggers. They talked to the leaders of the village and the leaders started to look very pleased. But they wouldn't say why. They said it was a secret, and that Salma and her friends must wait and see.

Salma could see that something was happening. Then the huge digging machines thundered about. Men with hard hats on shouted and pipes were put into the ground. Salma and her friends watched and wondered. Then at last it was finished. Everyone came to see.

The women from the village performed a special dance and the chief made a long speech which Salma thought was boring. "Hurry up and get on with it!" she whispered to herself.

The chief pulled a big metal handle up and down. And suddenly, Salma's eyes were wide with amazement. Clear, gushing water, right in the middle of the village. Everybody cheered. Salma tasted the water – it was delicious!

Life in the village was much better after that. Especially for the women, who never had to carry heavy jars of dirty water again.

8. Two types of **machine** are mentioned on page 18.
What are they?

9. What word tells you that the diggers were noisy?

10. Did the men talk quietly? ☐ **yes** ☐ **no**

11. Why do you think that is?

12. What did Salma think of the chief's speech?

☐ **special** ☐ **boring** ☐ **exciting**

13. How did the chief make water come out?

☐ **he turned the big tap**

☐ **he pulled the handle up and down**

☐ **it just gushed out by itself**

☐ **he got water from the well**

14. Why was life so much better for the women?

How to understand poetry

Poetry is very special in the way it uses words.
It uses words that **rhyme** and sentences that have **rhythm**.

A rhyme is when two words sound the same.
The rhyming words are underlined here.

One, two, three, four, <u>five</u>,
Once I caught a fish <u>alive</u>.
Six, seven, eight, nine, <u>ten</u>,
Then I let it go <u>again</u>.

Other words that rhyme are: **dive, hive; pen, men.**

The rhythm of the poem is the beat of the words in the sentence. Clap your hands on each beat of the word as you read this poem out loud.

Lon-don Bridge is fall-ing down,
Fall-ing down, fall-ing down.
Lon-don Bridge is fall-ing down,
My fair la-dy.

The Owl and the Pussy-Cat

The Owl and the Pussy-Cat went to sea
In a beautiful pea-green boat,
They took some honey, and plenty of money,
Wrapped up in a five-pound note.
The Owl looked up to the stars above,
And sang to a small guitar,
"O lovely Pussy! O Pussy, my love,
What a beautiful Pussy you are,
You are,
You are!
What a beautiful Pussy you are!"

1. Who went to sea?

____

____

2. Name two things about the boat.

____

____

3. What did they take to eat?

☐ **honey** ☐ **money**

☐ **peas**

4. Did you like this poem? Why?

____

____

How to understand non-fiction

The next few exercises are all **non-fiction**.
Remember: non-fiction is true and real, not made up.
Some of the exercises look different, but answer the questions in the same way.

Here are some things to remember when doing the following exercises:

An invitation is like a set of instructions.
It tells you what you are being invited to, the time and place and whether you should bring anything.

A recipe has a list and some instructions.
The **list** tells you everything you will need (the ingredients).
The **instructions** tell you what to do.

An encyclopedia is an information book. Everything is in a special order so you can easily look up what you want to know. Encyclopedias give you lots and lots of information.

It's Sam's 7th Birthday!
Please come to Waterland, Park Street, on Saturday 8th November.
2 o'clock – 4.30
Bring swimming things, including a towel.
Dear Sam,
I'd love to come to your party
I'm sorry I can't come to your party
From ....

1. Imagine that you can go to the party. Fill in the reply card.

2. How old will Sam be?

3. What sort of birthday party will it be?

4. What time will the party start?

☐	**4 o'clock**	☐	**Saturday 8th November**
☐	**2.30**	☐	**2 o'clock**

5. Name two things the guests must bring to the party.

Reading comprehension - non-fiction

Chocolate Biscuit Cake

Ingredients:
I packet digestive biscuits
75g butter
4 tablespoons cocoa powder
3 tablespoons syrup

1. Crush the biscuits into crumbs. Melt the butter in a large saucepan over a gentle heat.
2. Turn the heat off and mix the cocoa powder and syrup into the butter.
3. Pour the biscuit crumbs into the saucepan and mix well.
4. Tip the mixture into a greased, shallow tin and press down firmly all over. Put it in the fridge until it is hard. Cut into pieces.

I. What do you do with the biscuits?

☐ **melt them over a gentle heat** ☐ **crush them into crumbs**

☐ **mix the cocoa powder in** ☐ **cut them into pieces**

2. How much cocoa powder do you need?

☐ **75g** ☐ **4 tablespoons** ☐ **I packet**

3. Why does it tell you to use a large saucepan?

____

____

4. Which of these things is **not** needed in this recipe?

☐ **cocoa** ☐ **butter** ☐ **eggs**

Reading comprehension - non-fiction

Africa

Africa is the second largest continent after Asia. It contains over 50 countries. In the north there is a huge desert called the Sahara Desert. Further south are forests and grasslands where animals such as giraffes and elephants live. The River Nile is the longest river in the world. It is 6,741 kilometres (4,187 miles) long.

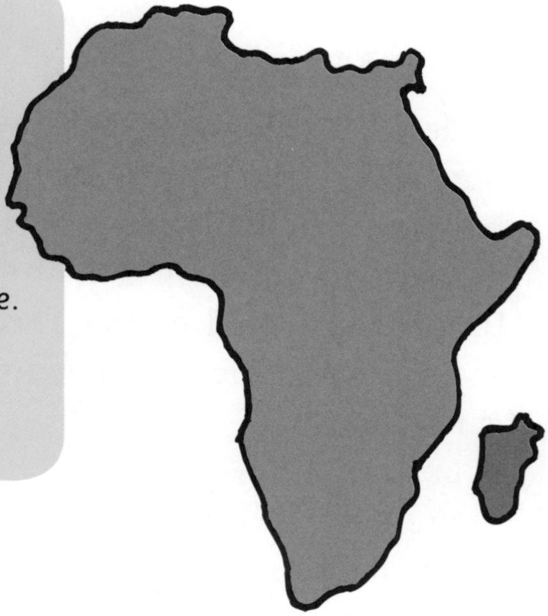

1. What is the largest continent?

2. Where, in Africa, is the Sahara Desert?

☐ **north** ☐ **south**

☐ **east** ☐ **west**

3. Name two animals that live in the south of Africa?

☐ **koala bears** ☐ **giraffes**

☐ **elephants** ☐ **squirrels**

4. How many miles long is the River Nile?

Reading comprehension - non-fiction

Deserts

A desert is a very dry land where there is hardly any rain. In the day, it can be so hot that you could fry an egg on the ground. But during the night it is sometimes so cold that water would freeze. This is because there are no clouds to keep the earth warm when the sun is not there.

Many deserts are covered in sand. But some have mountains, rocks, pebbles. The Great American Desert has cliffs that the wind has made into beautiful shapes. The Sahara Desert in Africa is mostly sand. The Australian Desert has red sand.

1. Why is a desert so dry?

☐ **because it is sandy** ☐ **because there is so little rain**

☐ **because the water is frozen** ☐ **because there are no clouds**

2. Is it always hot in a desert?

☐ **yes** ☐ **no**

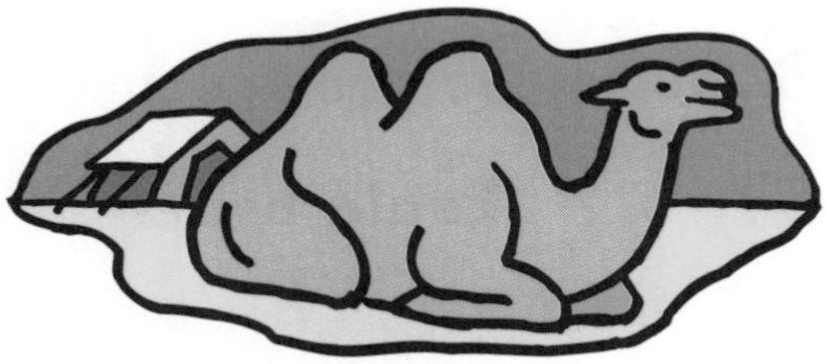

3. Which desert has beautiful rock shapes?

☐ **Australian** ☐ **Great American**

☐ **Sahara**

Reading comprehension - non-fiction

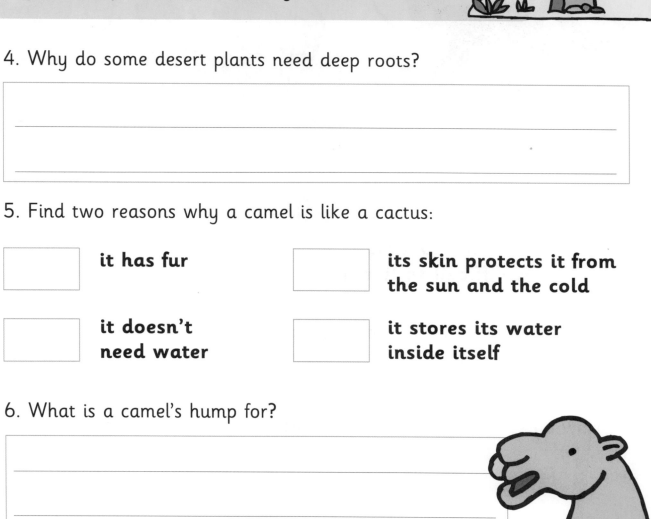

Sometimes it does not rain for a whole year in the desert. But there is water deep under the ground and some plants have roots that go very deep to find it.

One desert plant is the cactus, which has long, spreading roots. The cactus stores water inside its hard skin. This skin protects it from heat and cold.

Camels are a bit like cactus plants! They store water too – inside their humps. They have special fur that protects them from the sun during the day and keeps them warm at night.

4. Why do some desert plants need deep roots?

____

____

5. Find two reasons why a camel is like a cactus:

☐ **it has fur**

☐ **its skin protects it from the sun and the cold**

☐ **it doesn't need water**

☐ **it stores its water inside itself**

6. What is a camel's hump for?

____

____

Reading comprehension - non-fiction

Some other animals live in deserts, too. They have to be very good at seeing and hearing because most of them only come out at night. This is why many desert animals have extra-big eyes or ears.

A desert fox has bigger ears than a normal fox. A gerbil has huge eyes, so that it can see at night. It stays cool in the day by staying underground, like most desert animals.

Some animals don't drink at all. They get water from eating plants. The desert is very difficult to live in and only a few animals can survive there.

7. Why do desert animals have big eyes and ears?

- [ ] **because they live in a desert**
- [ ] **because they need to see and hear well at night**
- [ ] **because the desert is difficult to live in**
- [ ] **because they store water in them**

8. Why do most desert animals stay underground by day?

9. How do some animals manage without drinking at all?

Reading comprehension - non-fiction

Some people live in the desert but they always make their homes near an oasis. An oasis is where water comes from an underground stream.

Near an oasis, people can grow lots of plants and keep animals such as sheep and goats. They grow apricots, figs, olives, tea and rice.

Life is hard in the desert, for people, animals and plants. But desert people might think that our lives are hard, with our crowded streets and alarm clocks to wake us early every day!

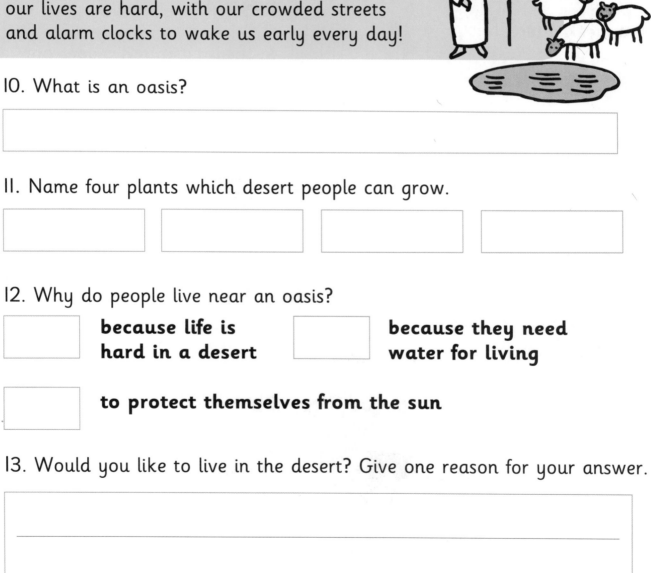

10. What is an oasis?

11. Name four plants which desert people can grow.

12. Why do people live near an oasis?

- [ ] **because life is hard in a desert**
- [ ] **because they need water for living**
- [ ] **to protect themselves from the sun**

13. Would you like to live in the desert? Give one reason for your answer.

page 7

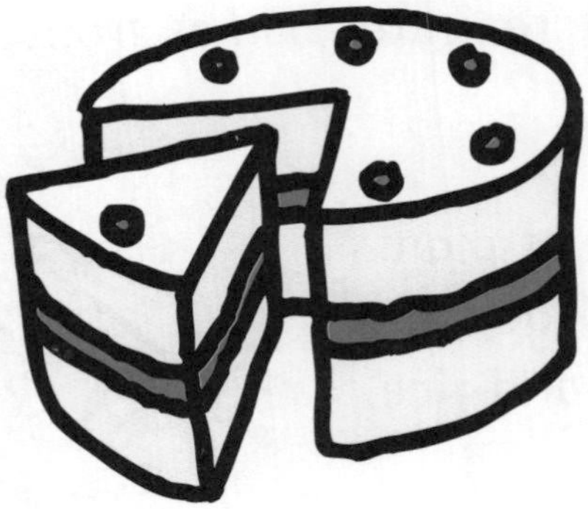

fiction
fiction
non-fiction
non-fiction

page 10

The Christmas Dog

1. a week after Christmas
2. Ben
3. he belongs/ed to someone else/ his owner would be missing him, NOT because they weren't allowed to/didn't have room

page 11

4. near the fire
5. because his owner didn't want him
6. pleased/delighted, etc
7. any relevant reason

page 12

The Big Surprise

1. in the garden shed
2. sometimes
3. anything showing that Jack was pleased, NOT because he wondered what it was

page 13

4. they put it in a bigger pot
5. because it was too big/had grown more/was almost as tall as Jack
6. nearly as tall as Jack
7. no

page 14

8. Jack and the Beanstalk
9. a giant
10. because he might fall

page 15

11. brown
12. because Jack shouted/yelled
13. at the flower show

page 16

Water, Lovely Water

1. hundreds of miles away

page 17

2. the market
3. clothes/oil/soap/tools
4. everyone
5. they had no water in the village/ nearby
6. all the women
7. they had been doing it for years AND water helped their food grow

page 19

8. trucks and diggers
9. thundered
10. no
11. so they could be heard/hear each other over the sound of the machines
12. boring
13. he pulled the handle up and down
14. they wouldn't have to carry heavy jars/anything about the women not having to do this work again

page 21

1. the Owl and the Pussy-Cat
2. it was beautiful AND it was pea-green
3. honey

4. any reasonable answer

Answers

page 23

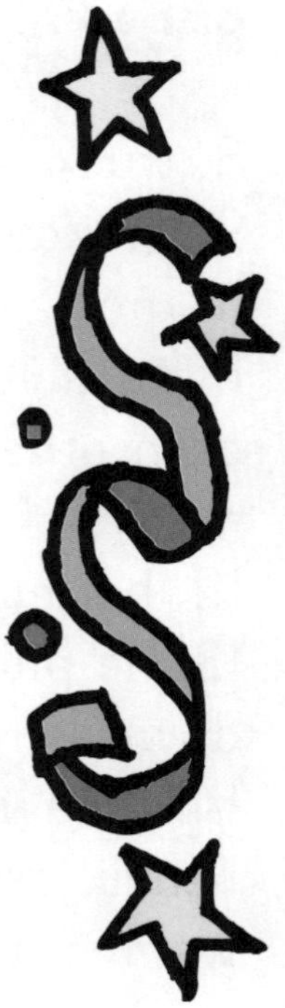

1. correct box should be ticked/crossed and name should be written in the space
2. 7/seven
3. swimming
4. 2 o'clock
5. swimming costume/ trunks/towel/anything needed for swimming

page 24

1. crush them into crumbs
2. 4 tablespoons
3. so there's enough room for the biscuits/so that it's big enough NOT to melt the butter
4. eggs

page 25

1. Asia
2. north
3. giraffes and elephants
4. 4,187 miles NOT 6,741 kilometres

page 26

Deserts

1. because there is so little rain
2. no
3. Great American

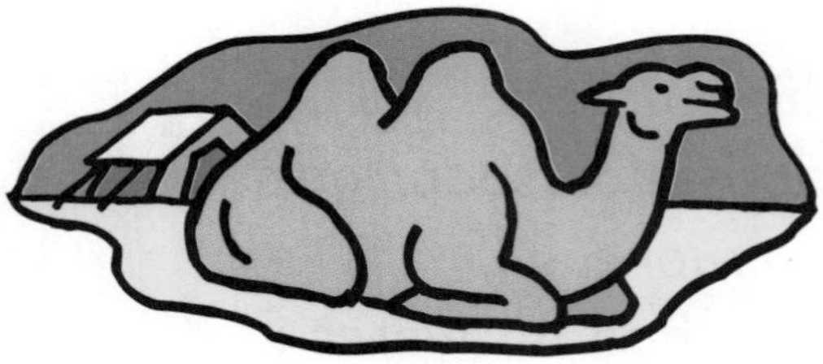

page 27

4. because there is water underground/to suck water from deep underground
5. its skin protects it from the sun and the cold AND it stores water inside itself
6. storing water

page 28

7. because they need to see and hear well at night
8. to stay cool/to keep out of the heat/sun
9. they get water from eating plants/by eating plants with water in

page 29

10. a place where water comes from underground/ where there is water in the desert
11. apricots/figs/olives/tea/rice
12. because they need water for living
13. any reasonable answer which shows understanding of the passage

How did you do?

Words you have learnt

comprehension
sentence
capital letter
full stop

fiction
pretend
made up
story
adventure story
ghost story
fairy story
love story
poem
(poet)
rhyme
rhythm

non-fiction
real
true
encyclopedia
newspaper
textbook
map
recipe
list
instruction
fact
invitation

Checklist

After working through each section, put a tick in the box to show how you feel about the topic.

If you tick 'Not sure' go back to those pages and try again.

	Confident	Not sure
The Christmas Dog		
The Big Surprise		
Water, Lovely Water		
The Owl and the Pussy-Cat		
Invitation		
Recipe		
Encyclopedia		
Deserts		

How to spell in different ways

Learning to spell can be tricky, but if you remember a few basic rules and learn these slowly you will get there!

Words fall into two groups when it comes to spelling.

1. **Pattern words**
- car, far, start
- fight, tight, frightened

These words have the same spelling patterns.

2. **Sight words**
- said, their, one, many, does

These words don't share a spelling pattern.
You have to learn these by sight.

Pattern words are easy to spell because once you learn the pattern you can spell a whole group of words.
Here are some words with spelling patterns – the patterns have been underlined in each word.
mug, dug, lug and jug all have the pattern **ug**.
toast, goat, throat and boat all have the pattern **oa**.
think, sink, drink and wink all have the pattern **ink**.

Different ways to spell

Circle the bit that's the same in each of these words.

car **far** **start** **dart**

Look at these words and circle the bit that's the same in each.

boat **float** **coat** **oat** **moat**

Now cover them up and spell these.

_ _ _ _

_ _ _ _

Take a look at these words and circle the bit that's the same in each.

fight **sight** **right** **tight** **light**

How do you spell the word that means the opposite of day? ____________________

How to spell with word beginnings

Lots of words have a spelling pattern at the **beginning** of the word.

Sometimes this might be two consonants together:

dr **gr** **cr** **fr** **br** **tr**

These letters are called a **consonant cluster**.
The consonants often appear together to make lots of useful words.

Remember:
Vowels are **a, e, i, o, u.**
All the other letters of the alphabet are called consonants!

Patterns of word beginnings

Spell each word by looking at the picture and slotting in the letters. Write the word again underneath for practice.

fr

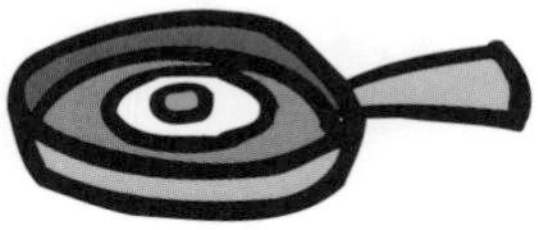

_ _ y

_ _ _

_ _ o s t

_ _ _ _ _

_ _ o g

_ _ _ _

br

_ _ i d g e

_ _ _ _ _ _

_ _ i c k

_ _ _ _ _

_ _ i m

_ _ _ _

tr

_ _ e e

_ _ _ _

_ _ i c k

_ _ _ _ _

_ _ a i n

_ _ _ _ _

Patterns of word beginnings

Here are some more consonant clusters.

dr

_ _ e s s

_ _ _ _ _

_ _ a w

_ _ _ _

_ _ i p

_ _ _ _

gr

_ _ a p e

_ _ _ _ _

_ _ o w

_ _ _ _

_ _ a s s

_ _ _ _ _

cr

_ _ a b

_ _ _ _

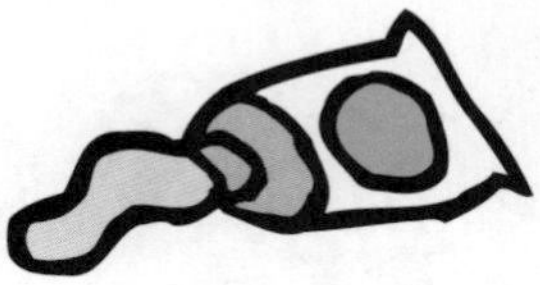

_ _ e a m

_ _ _ _ _

_ _ y

_ _ _

Patterns of word beginnings

Time for some extra practice!

cl

_ _ o w n

_ _ _ _ _

_ _ a w

_ _ _ _

_ _ o u d

_ _ _ _ _

pl

_ _ a n e t

_ _ _ _ _ _

_ _ u m

_ _ _ _

_ _ a n t

_ _ _ _ _

fl

_ _ a g

_ _ _ _

_ _ a m e

_ _ _ _ _

_ _ o w e r

_ _ _ _ _ _

How to spell with word endings

Lots of words have a spelling pattern at the **end** of a word.

Just like you have seen at the beginning of words, these are consonant clusters too.

ck

ng

nd

lp

st

nk

Patterns at the end of words

Do the letter sums to spell the **ck** words.
Draw lines to match the words to the pictures.

du	+	ck	=	_ _ _ _
so	+	ck	=	_ _ _ _
ki	+	ck	=	_ _ _ _
sa	+	ck	=	_ _ _ _
ne	+	ck	=	_ _ _ _

The letters **ng** come at the end of words.

Write the words that finish the sentences.
Choose from the list.

thing **king** **bang** **ring** **sing** **rang**

The _ _ _ _ ruled all the land.

Sarah got a _ _ _ _ for her birthday.

Ben is in the choir. He likes to _ _ _ _ .

The phone _ _ _ _ so I answered it.

Patterns at the end of words

Do the letter sums to spell the **nd** words.

a + nd = _ _ _

ha + nd = _ _ _ _

be + nd = _ _ _ _

ba + nd = _ _ _ _

se + nd = _ _ _ _

sta + nd = _ _ _ _ _

The letters **lp** come at the end of words.

Write the words that finish the sentences.
Choose from the list.

pulp **gulp** **scalp** **help** **yelp**

Jimmy took a big _ _ _ _ of his orange juice.

Karen decided to _ _ _ _ her mum with the shopping.

The puppy let out a _ _ _ _ when the postman walked up the path.

Patterns at the end of words

Do the letter sums to spell the **st** words.

be	+	st	=	_ _ _ _
fa	+	st	=	_ _ _ _
la	+	st	=	_ _ _ _
bla	+	st	=	_ _ _ _ _
che	+	st	=	_ _ _ _ _
fore	+	st	=	_ _ _ _ _ _

The letters **nk** come at the end of words.

Write the words that finish the sentences.
Choose from the list.

sink **bank** **blink** **shrunk** **think**

Hannah put her pocket money in the _ _ _ _ .

When Joe took his T-shirt out of the washing machine it had _ _ _ _ _ _ .

Harold began to _ _ _ _ _ about his summer holiday.

How to make plurals

A **singular** word tells you about **one** thing.

A **plural** word tells you about **more than one thing**.

There are different ways to turn a singular into a plural.
The most common way is to add an **s** on the end of the word.

apple	apple**s**	bike	bike**s**

Some plurals are spelt by adding **es** to the end of the word.
These words usually end in **ss**, **ch**, **x** or **sh**.

dress	dress**es**	watch	watch**es**
fox	fox**es**	dish	dish**es**

Words that end with a **y** make plurals in two different ways, either by adding **s** or **ies**.

day	day**s**	pony	pon**ies**
ray	ray**s**	story	stor**ies**

Some words change altogether,
and some don't change at all!

child	**children**
sheep	**sheep**

Plurals

Look at the singular words.
Spell the plural word underneath each one.

Plurals with s

day hand cup insect

_ _ _ _   _ _ _ _ _   _ _ _ _   _ _ _ _ _ _ _

cooker doll panda

_ _ _ _ _ _ _   _ _ _ _ _   _ _ _ _ _ _

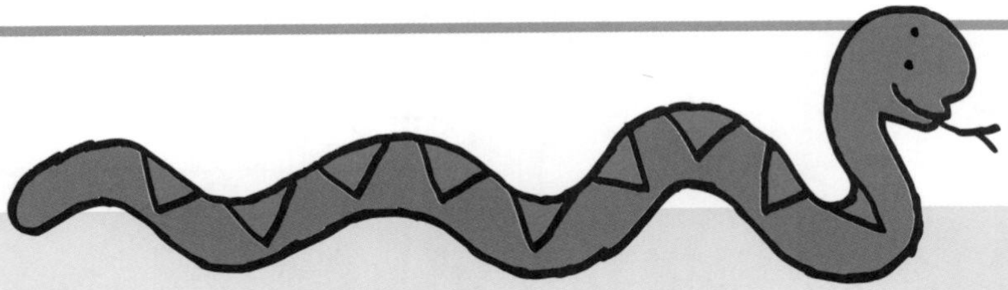

Plurals with es

witch kiss fox box

_ _ _ _ _ _ _   _ _ _ _ _ _   _ _ _ _ _   _ _ _ _ _

bush wish match

_ _ _ _ _ _   _ _ _ _ _ _   _ _ _ _ _ _ _

Plurals

There are two ways of spelling the plurals for words ending in **y**.

vowel + y = s → boy → boys

consonant + y = ies → baby → babies

Spell the plural for these words.

s	
bay	_ _ _ _
tray	_ _ _ _ _
toy	_ _ _ _
key	_ _ _ _

ies	
pony	_ _ _ _ _ _
nappy	_ _ _ _ _ _ _
puppy	_ _ _ _ _ _ _
fairy	_ _ _ _ _ _ _

Now take a look at these words ending in **y**.
Look closely at the letter **before** the **y** and decide whether the plural is **s** or **ies**.

Singular	**Plural**
party	____________
poppy	____________
play	____________
day	____________

Plurals

The plural spellings for some words do not follow any rules.
Each box has a choice of plural spellings for each word.
Circle the correct spelling and then write it underneath.

sheep

sheeps

sheepies

sheep

_ _ _ _ _

tooth

teeth

tooths

toothes

_ _ _ _ _

woman

womanes

women

womans

_ _ _ _ _

child

childies

childes

children

_ _ _ _ _ _ _ _

man

men

mans

manies

_ _ _

50 How to spell different sounds

Spelling is a way of using letters to show sounds.
Unfortunately, in English, not every sound is spelt the same way.

Look at this example.

Read these words out loud and listen to their sounds.

br**ough**t
alth**ough**
t**ough**
pl**ough**
thr**ough**

These words have the same **ough** spelling pattern, but the letters make a completely different sound in each word.

Now look at this example.

Read these words out loud and listen to their sounds.

boat
slow
hole

These words all have a different spelling pattern but they make the same sound!

Sound patterns

Here is a sound to listen for.

Write these words with **ee**.

Too many sw _ _ _ _ are bad for your teeth.

The king and qu _ _ _ spent a w _ _ _ at their castle.

Your f _ _ _ smell really bad!

Write these words with **ea**.

I let an old lady sit on my s _ _ _ on the bus.

I made sure my bedroom was n _ _ _ and tidy.

Mum took us to the fair for a tr _ _ _ .

So, **ee** and **ea** can have the same sound!

Look at these pictures and spell each word correctly.

_ _ _ _ _

_ _ _ _ _

_ _ _ _

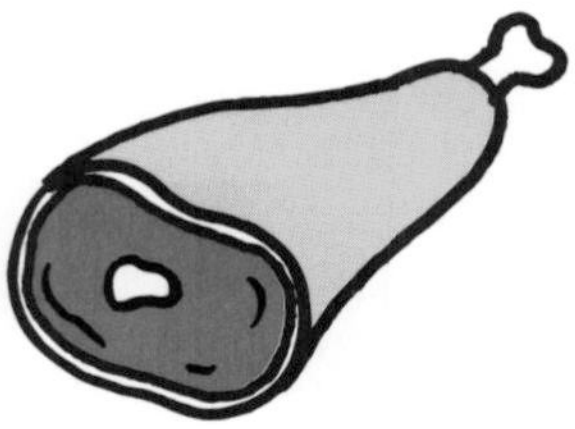

_ _ _ _

Sound patterns

Here is another sound.
Write these words with **oa**.

I can't speak I have a sore t _ _ _ _ _ .

Does ice sink or f _ _ _ _ ?

This sound can also be spelt with **ow**.
Write these words with **ow**.

The infants performed a s _ _ _ for the juniors.

I put my tooth under my p _ _ _ _ _ for the tooth fairy.

Another spelling for this sound is **o_e**.
Write these words with **o_e**.

My dad hit the golf ball into the h _ _ _ .

After going on holiday it's always nice to go back h _ _ _ .

Look at these pictures and spell each word correctly.

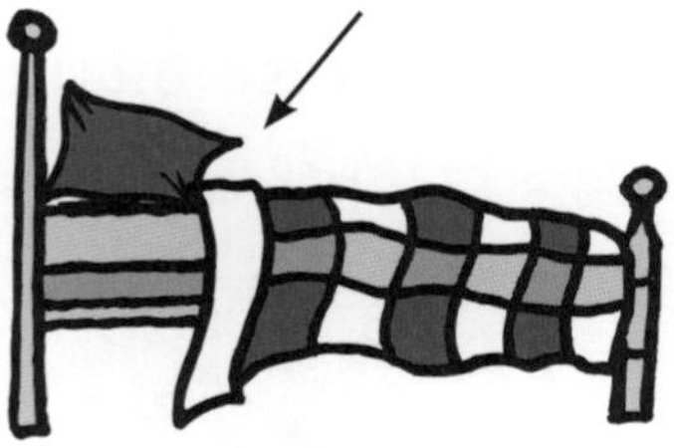

_ _ _ _   _ _ _ _   _ _ _ _ _ _

Sound patterns

Here is a different sound to listen for.
Write these words with **ie**.

I told a l _ _ to my teacher. She was very cross.

For tea we ate steak and kidney p _ _ .

Now write these words with **igh**.

The opposite of day is n _ _ _ _ .

The box was too h _ _ _ up for me to reach.

Write these words with **y**.

The birds decided to f _ _ south for the winter.

W _ _ did the chicken cross the road?

Look at these pictures and spell each word correctly.

_ _ _ _ _

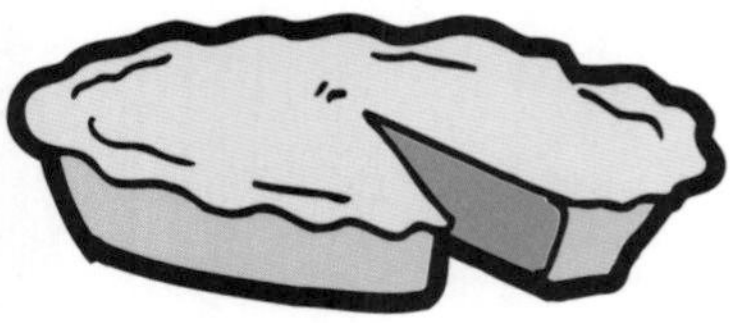

_ _ _

_ _ _

How to spell other patterns

Some spelling patterns always appear in the same place in a word.

Example:

boy	soil	**oy** and **oi** sound the same.
toy	boil	
bay	train	**ay** and **ai** sound the same.
say	snail	

Rules:

Never use **oi** at the end of a word.
It always goes in the middle of English words.

Never use **ai** at the end of a word.
It always goes in the middle of English words.

If you hear an **oy** sound at the **end** of a word, write **oy**.
If you hear an **ay** sound at the **end** of a word, write **ay**.

Sound patterns at the beginning and end of words

Look at these words.

point boil spoil toy
enjoy destroy annoy

Write the correct words in the spaces.

1. You will ________ me if you ________ my ________.
2. Don't ________ the soup or you will ________ it.
3. I don't ________ it when you ________ at me.

See if you can complete these words with **oi** or **oy**.

n _ _ s e

b _ _

j _ _

j _ _ n t

t o m b _ _

t o r t _ _ s e

Sound patterns at the beginning and end of words

Complete these words with **ai** or **ay**.

p _ _ n t

t r _ _ n

p l _ _

s n _ _ l

t r _ _

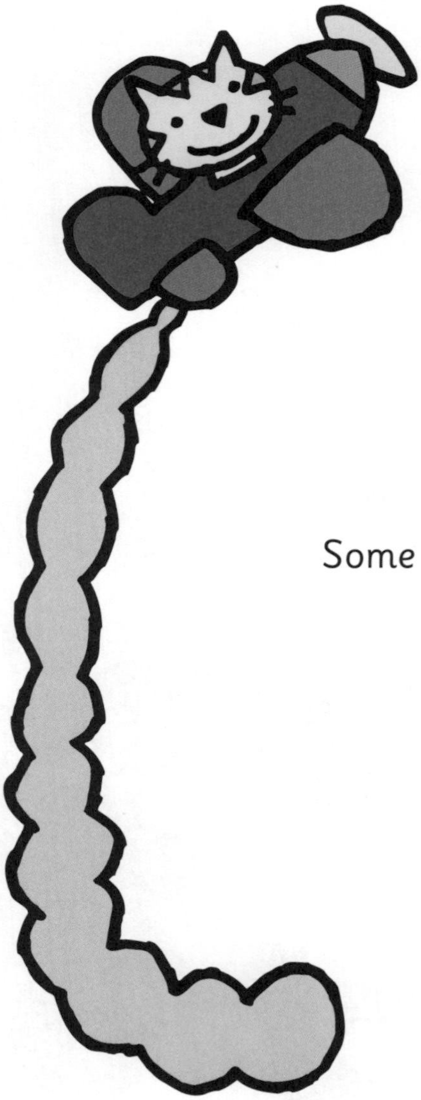

Some more words to complete with **ai** or **ay**.

f _ _ n t

s w _ _

c l _ _

w _ _ s t

s t _ _

Sound patterns at the beginning and end of words

How many words can you make using these letter combinations?

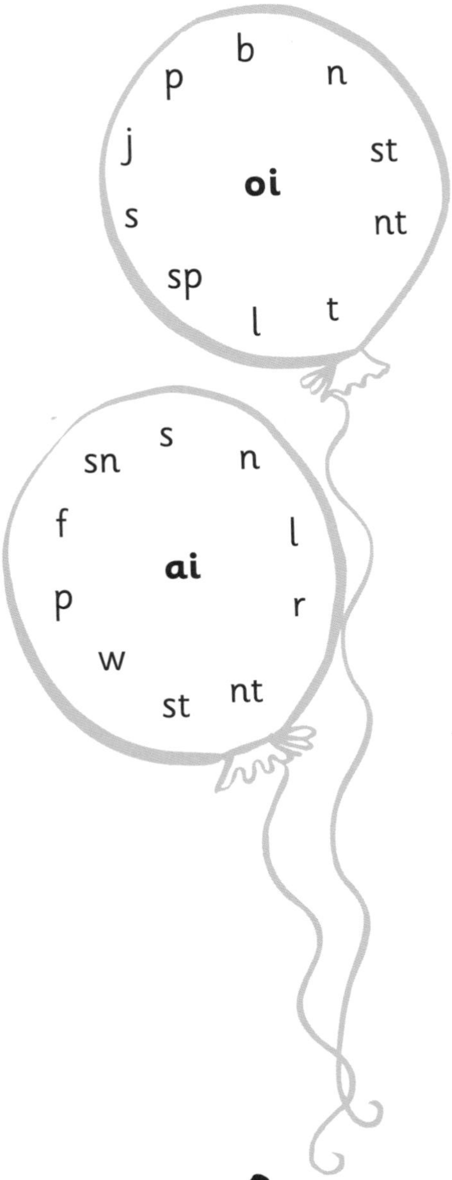

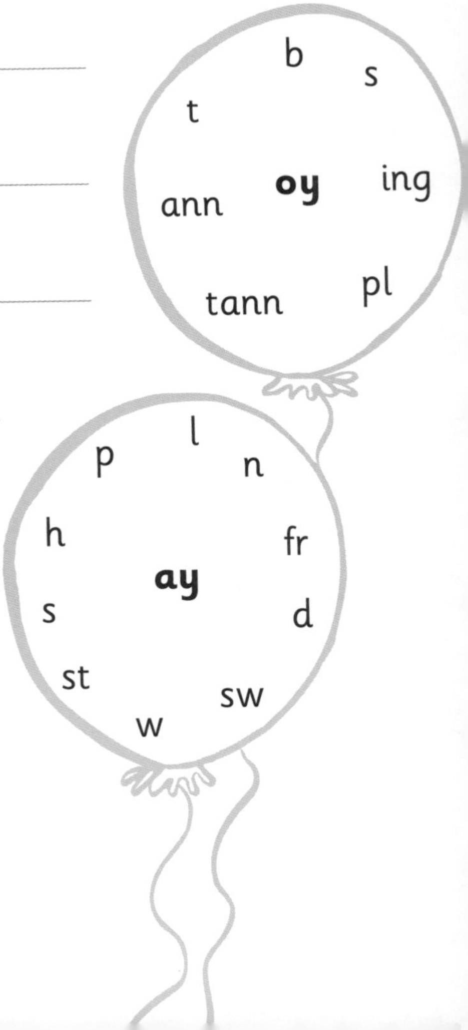

How to add ing and ed to words

Adding **ing** or **ed** to a word makes a brand new word.
Here are some of the rules you will need to learn.

There are three ways to add **ing** to a word.

1. Just add **ing**.
sing + ing = singing

2. If the word ends in **e**, lose the **e** before adding **ing**.
give + ing = giving

3. Double the last letter.
hop + ing = hopping

There are three ways to add **ed** to a word.

1. Just add **ed**.
walk + ed = walked

2. If the word ends in **e**, lose the extra **e** before adding **ed**.
dance + ed = danced

3. Double the last letter.
shop + ed = shopped

Adding ing and ed

Here is a long list of words!

Add **ing** to them and remember to double the last letter.

win	w i n n i n g
clap	_ _ _ _ _ _ _ _
sip	_ _ _ _ _ _ _
hop	_ _ _ _ _ _ _
get	_ _ _ _ _ _ _
swim	_ _ _ _ _ _ _ _
cut	_ _ _ _ _ _ _
shop	_ _ _ _ _ _ _ _
run	_ _ _ _ _ _ _

Adding ing and ed

Spell these words by adding **ing**.
Watch out if the word ends in **e**!

read	r e a d i n g
look	_ _ _ _ _ _ _
smile	_ _ _ _ _ _ _
eat	_ _ _ _ _ _
wave	_ _ _ _ _ _
take	_ _ _ _ _ _
come	_ _ _ _ _ _
bite	_ _ _ _ _ _
sleep	_ _ _ _ _ _ _ _

Spell these words by adding **ed**.
Watch out if the word ends in **e**!
You may need to double the last letter.

look	l o o k e d
watch	_ _ _ _ _ _ _
jump	_ _ _ _ _ _
laugh	_ _ _ _ _ _ _
climb	_ _ _ _ _ _ _
clap	_ _ _ _ _ _ _
share	_ _ _ _ _ _
hop	_ _ _ _ _ _
dare	_ _ _ _ _

Adding ing and ed

Finish the stories below with **ing** and **ed** words.
The words to use have been given to help you.

(walk)
Yesterday I w __ __ __ __ __ up a big hill with my dad.
(climb)
We c __ __ __ __ __ __ up a very steep rock. I could see
(swim)
children s __ __ __ __ __ __ __ in the lake below. Some
(sit)
people were s __ __ __ __ __ __ at the side of the lake.

(shop)
Last Saturday, I went s __ __ __ __ __ __ __ with my
(walk)
mum. On the way to the bus stop we w __ __ __ __ __
(cut)
past a hairdresser's. A lady was c __ __ __ __ __ __
(laugh)
a little girl's hair. We couldn't stop l __ __ __ __ __ __ __
(pull)
because the girl was p __ __ __ __ __ __ a really

grumpy face!

How to spell ph and wh words

When **p** and **h** go together they make the sound **f**.
Read these words and listen to the sound **ph** makes.

phone
photo
phrase
tro**ph**y
gra**ph**
geogra**ph**y

The letters **wh** sound like 'w'. The letter **h** is 'silent', which means you only make the 'w' sound.
A lot of **wh** words are question words:

what?
why?
where?
when?
who?

You need to learn which words are spelt with **ph** and which with f.
You also need to learn when a 'w' word has a silent 'h'.

There are no rules – you just have to learn them!

Spelling ph and wh words

Read the words below.

Philip took a photo
of a dolphin saying the
whole alphabet
to an elephant!

Christopher won a trophy
when he took a photo
of a pheasant on the phone!

Can you spell all the **ph** words you can see on this page?
The first two are done for you.

Philip ______ photo ______ ______

______ ______ ______

______ ______ ______

Spelling ph and wh words

Write **ph** to spell the words.
Spell the words twice more.
Match the words to the pictures.

_ _ o t o   _ _ _ _ _   _ _ _ _ _

g r a _ _   _ _ _ _ _   _ _ _ _ _

_ _ o n e   _ _ _ _ _   _ _ _ _ _

Spell the correct **ph** words in the spaces.
Choose from the words below.

alphabet	photos
pheasant	phone

I took lots of _ _ _ _ _ _ _ on holiday.

My mum keeps on telling me to get off the _ _ _ _ _ !

My grandma doesn't eat turkey on Christmas day,
she eats _ _ _ _ _ _ _ _ _ _ instead.

I can say the _ _ _ _ _ _ _ _ _ backwards!

Spelling ph and wh words

Write **wh** to spell the words.
Draw circles around the words that ask questions.
The first one has been done for you.

_ _ eel   (w h y)   _ _ at   _ _ ite

_ _ en   _ _ ere   _ _ ich   _ _ isper

Write **wh** to spell the words.
Choose and spell each one to finish the questions.

_ _ o   _ _ at   _ _ ere   _ _ en   _ _ y   _ _ ich

_ _ _ _ _ of these buns do you want?

_ _ _ _ is the answer?

_ _ _ _ _ are you going to?

_ _ _ is hiding?

_ _ _ do balls bounce?

_ _ _ _ is your birthday?

How to learn sight words

Some words are odd to learn because they don't have a spelling pattern. These words have to be learned by sight because they have difficult spellings.

Here is a useful method to help you learn tricky sight words.

Look **Say** **Cover** **Write** **Check**

Follow each step, one by one, and you'll be able to spell any word you can think of!

1. **Look** at the word.
2. **Say** the letters out loud.
3. **Cover** the word.
4. **Write** it from memory.
5. **Check** by uncovering the word.

Learn to spell these sight words using the **look**, **say**, **cover**, **write**, **check** method.

do	_ _
their	_ _ _ _ _
many	_ _ _ _
said	_ _ _ _
beautiful	_ _ _ _ _ _ _ _ _
when	_ _ _ _
come	_ _ _ _
they	_ _ _ _
because	_ _ _ _ _ _ _
people	_ _ _ _ _ _
house	_ _ _ _ _
would	_ _ _ _ _
went	_ _ _ _

How to understand syllables

Syllables are the number of parts in a word that you can hear when you say a word.

Example:

The word **today** has two syllables because you can hear two parts of the word when you say it.

today
to day
(1) (2)

Try saying the word slowly and clapping your hands for each bit.

If you play a musical instrument or like listening to music, the syllables are like the beats that you can hear.

Some words have more than two syllables.

Saturday
Sat – ur – day
(1) (2) (3)

candyfloss
can – dy – floss
(1) (2) (3)

Knowing about syllables can help you with spelling because you can break words up into smaller parts to spell.

Syllables

These puzzles contain words split into syllables.

Join each jigsaw piece to another to make a word.
Then write the word.

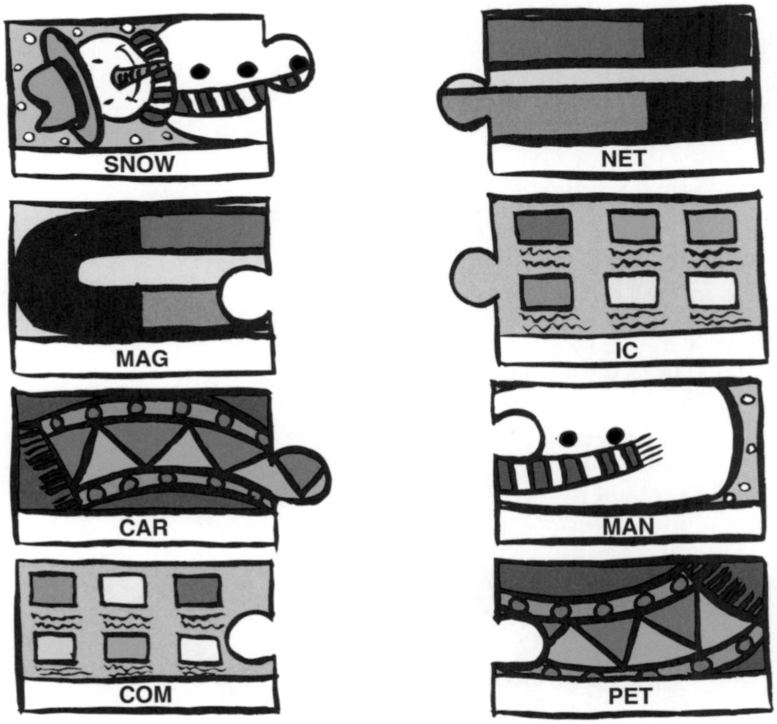

Here are some bits of words. Match the parts of the word to make a new word and write it on the line. The first one has been done for you.

hand	sent	
sis	dy	
pre	bag	handbag
ted	lo	
hel	ter	

70 Syllables

Let's practise words with more than one syllable.

Can you spell these words by breaking them into syllables? The first one has been done for you.

inside	looking	about
i n / s i d e	_ _ _ _ _ _ _	_ _ _ _ _
banker	terrible	telescope
_ _ _ _ _ _	_ _ _ _ _ _ _ _	_ _ _ _ _ _ _ _ _
holiday	policeman	sister
_ _ _ _ _ _ _	_ _ _ _ _ _ _ _ _	_ _ _ _ _ _

Now choose four of those words and learn them, using

LOOK, **SAY**, **COVER**, **WRITE**, **CHECK**.

1. ____________________
2. ____________________
3. ____________________
4. ____________________

Syllables

Read each word, then cover it up quickly.
See if you can spell it and mark where each syllable ends.
Then check it and underline any bits you got wrong.

annoying natural Saturday

__________ __________ __________

asteroid talented acrobatic

__________ __________ __________

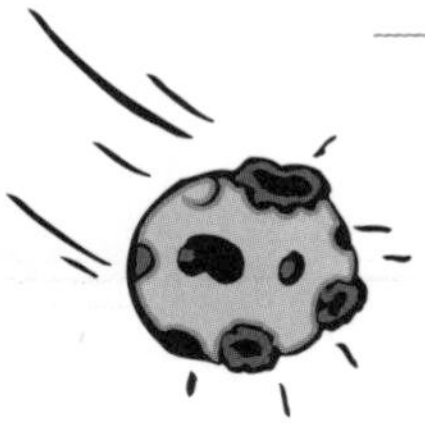

Choose three words to learn, using

LOOK, **SAY**, **COVER**, **WRITE**, **CHECK**.

When you SAY the letters, shout or sing the bit you got wrong!
This will help you remember.

1. __________
2. __________
3. __________

Spelling pictures

Spell these words that are in the picture.

Spell these words that are in the picture.

Answers

page 37

car, far, start, dart
boat, float, coat, oat,
moat coat, boat
fight, sight, right, tight
light, night

page 39

fry
frost
frog

bridge
brick
brim

tree
trick
train

page 40

dress
draw
drip

grape
grow
grass

crab
cream
cry

page 41

clown
claw
cloud

planet
plum
plant

flag
flame
flower

page 43

duck, sock, kick,
sack, neck

The king ruled all the land.
Sarah got a ring for her birthday.
Ben is in the choir. He likes to sing.
The phone rang so I answered it.

page 44

and
hand
bend
band
send
stand

Jimmy took a big gulp of
his orange juice.
Karen decided to help her mum
with the shopping.
The puppy let out a yelp when
the postman walked up the path.

page 45

best
fast
last
blast
chest
forest

Hannah put her pocket money in the bank.
When Joe took his T-shirt out of the washing machine it had shrunk.
Harold began to think about his summer holiday.

page 47

days, hands, cups, insects, cookers, dolls, pandas

witches, kisses, foxes, boxes, bushes,

wishes, matches

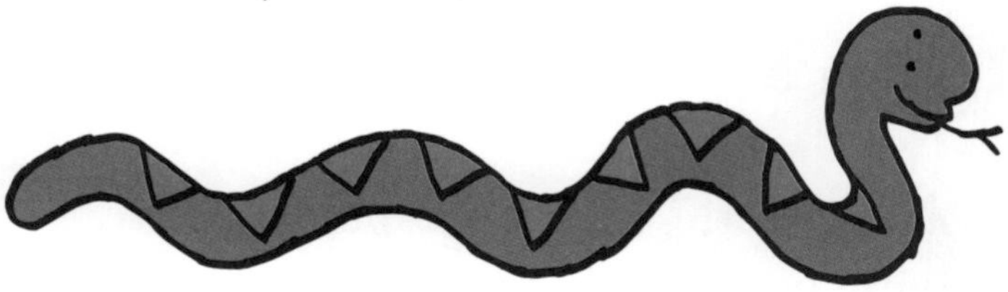

page 48

bays, trays, toys, keys

ponies, nappies, puppies, fairies

parties, poppies, plays, days

page 59

sheep
teeth
women
children
men

page 51

Too many sweets are bad for your teeth.
The king and queen spent a week at their castle.
Your feet smell really bad!

I let an old lady sit on my seat on the bus.
I made sure my bedroom was neat and tidy.
Mum took us to the fair for a treat.
sweet, queen, seat, meat

Answers

page 52

I can't speak. I have a sore throat.
Does ice sink or float?
The infants performed a show for the juniors.
I put my tooth under my pillow for the tooth fairy.
My dad hit the golf ball into the hole.
After going on holiday it is always nice to go back home.

boat, coat, pillow

page 53

I told a lie to my teacher. She was very cross.
For tea we ate steak and kidney pie.
The opposite of day is night.
The box was too high up for me to reach.
The birds decided to fly south for the winter.
Why did the chicken cross the road?

night, pie, tie

page 55

1. You will annoy me if you destroy my toy.
2. Don't boil the soup or you will spoil it.
3. I don't enjoy it when you point at me.

noise
boy
joy
joint
tomboy
tortoise

page 56

paint
train
play
snail
tray

faint
sway
clay
waist
stay

page 57

Accept any correctly spelt words with oi, oy, ay, and ai.

page 59

clapping
sipping
hopping
getting
swimming
cutting
shopping
running

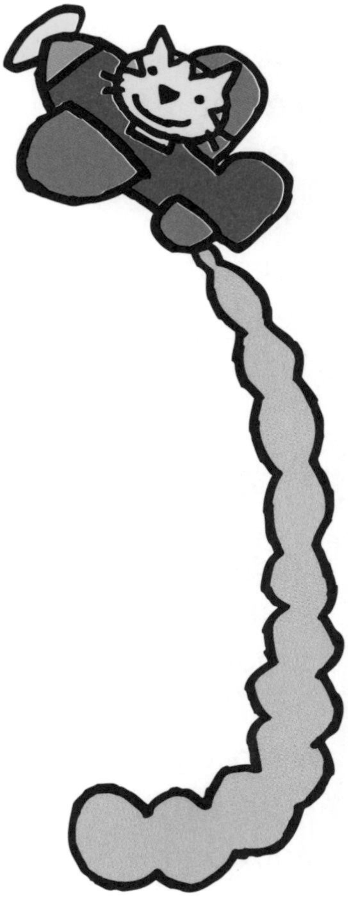

page 60

looking
smiling
eating
waving
taking
coming
biting
sleeping

watched
jumped
laughed
climbed
clapped
shared
hopped
dared

page 61

Yesterday I walked up a big hill with my dad. We climbed up a very steep rock. I could see children swimming in the lake below. Some people were sitting at the side of the lake.

Last Saturday, I went shopping with my mum. On the way to the bus stop we walked past a hairdresser's. A lady was cutting a little girl's hair. We couldn't stop laughing because the girl was pulling a really grumpy face!

page 63

dolphin
alphabet
elephant
Christopher
trophy
pheasant
phone

page 64

photo, graph, phone
I took lots of photos on holiday.
My mum keeps telling me to get off the phone!
My grandma doesn't eat turkey on Christmas day, she eats pheasant instead.
I can say the alphabet backwards!

page 65

wheel, why, what, white, when, where, which, whisper
words that ask questions:
why, what, when, where, which

who, what, where, when, why, which
Which of these buns do you want?
What is the answer?
Where are you going to?
Who is hiding?
Why do balls bounce?
When is your birthday?

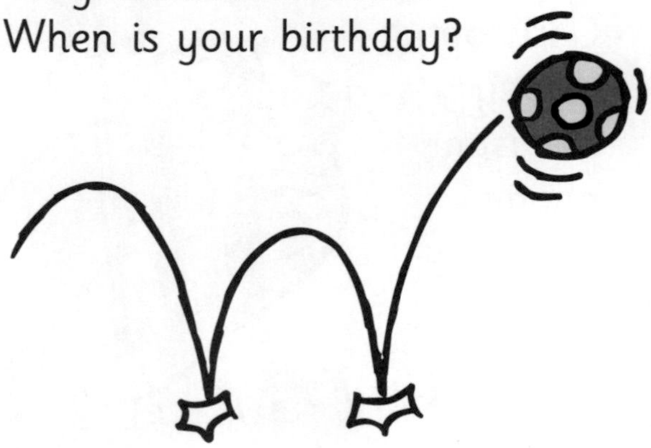

page 69

snowman
magnet
carpet
comic

sister
present
teddy
hello

page 70

in/side
look/ing
a/bout
ban/ker
ter/ri/ble
tel/e/scope
hol/i/day
pol/ice/man
sis/ter

Your child may break the syllables at different points.

page 71

a/nnoy/ing
nat/u/ral
Sat/ur/day
as/ter/oid
ta/len/ted
a/cro/ba/tic

page 72

1. shell
2. boat or ship
3. flag
4. boy
5. sun
6. sand
7. waves or sea

page 73

1. pipe
2. dog
3. moon
4. snowman
5. bird
6. tree
7. scarf
8. hat

Words you have learnt

letter

sounds

word

consonant

consonant cluster

vowel

singular

plural

spelling pattern

syllable

pattern words

sight words

Checklist

After working through each section, put a tick in the box to show how you feel about the topic.

If you tick 'Not sure' go back to those pages and try again.

	Confident	Not sure
Pattern words		
Sight words		
Beginning spellings		
End spellings		
Plurals		
Spelling different sounds		
Spelling **oi**, **oy**, **ai**, **ay**		
Adding **ing** and **ed**		
Words with **ph** and **wh**		
Syllables		
Spelling pictures		

How to do writing composition

Before you try the writing exercises in this book,
think hard about the following things:

• If you want to write a long word but don't know how to spell it, 'sound out' the bits (syllables) of the word one at a time.
Example: adventurous **ad-ven-chu-rus**
Then ask a parent to help you or look in the dictionary for the right spelling.

• Don't start all your sentences in the same way.
Example: I went to school in the morning. Then I had my lunch on the field. Then I had my afternoon lessons. Then I went home.
Think of different words to 'then' – next, after, etc, to make your writing more interesting.

• Make sure that **every** sentence starts with a **capital letter** and ends in a **full stop**.
A sentence is a collection of words that makes sense.
If it doesn't make sense it isn't a sentence.

Sentence	**Not a sentence**
The baby has no hair.	The baby hair.
My grandma is deaf.	My grandma is.
The water was deep.	Water was deep.

Writing composition

Start by writing a story about yourself. Include information about your friends and family and where you live. You could also write about your favourite pop group or hobby.

How to understand character

The people or animals in a story are called the **characters**.

When you write a story, think very carefully about your characters:

- what they look like
- where they live
- what sort of person they are

This is the beginning of the fairy tale 'Cinderella'.

Read it and see how the writer has described the main character.

Cinderella

There was once a girl called Cinderella who wore old, torn, shabby clothes. She was a very shy girl and did what she was told. Cinderella's wicked stepmother made her do all the dirty work in the house. She washed the floors and dusted the bedrooms. Cinderella obediently helped to dress her two sisters for the ball at the palace. She wished them to have a good time.

Here are some notes about the character:

Name	What they look like	What sort of person
Cinderella	wears old, torn, shabby clothes	very shy, obedient does what she is told

Here's an example of how the story can change if we change the notes about the character.

Name	What they look like	What sort of person
Glimmerbell	wears elegant, silky, expensive clothes	very confident disobedient mean spoilt

Glimmerbell

There was once a girl called Glimmerbell who wore elegant, silky, expensive clothes. She was a very confident girl and never did what she was told. Glimmerbell's wicked stepmother made her do all the dirty work in the house. But Glimmerbell refused to and had a tantrum every time she was asked. Glimmerbell made her sisters dress themselves for the ball at the palace. She told them she hoped no one would dance with them!

The story has really changed!
So the way you describe your character is very important in your story.

Thinking about your characters carefully can really make your story very exciting and interesting.

Character

Here are some different notes for the Cinderella character.
Choose a few of the descriptions to make up your own new character for the story.
Once you have chosen them, write them in the spaces below.

Name	What they look like	What sort of person
Jollyella	tall and slim	happy
Mousey	scruffy	shy
Moodykins	tiny	grumpy
Raggabella	always smiling	lazy
	always frowning	quiet
	wears smart, clean clothes	loud
	wears old, ragged clothes	naughty
	wears brightly coloured clothes	

Name	What they look like	What sort of person
____________	____________	____________
	____________	____________
	____________	____________
	____________	____________
	____________	____________
	____________	____________

Character

Now fill in the story describing **your** new character.
Make sure your story makes sense. If you describe your character as quiet then don't have them shouting at everyone! Look back at the story on page 84 to help you.

(The name of your character)

____

There was once a girl called

____________________ who wore

____

clothes. She was a very ________

girl and _________ did what she

was told. ___________________'s

wicked stepmother made her do all

the dirty work in the house.

____

____

____

____

for the ball at the palace. ______

____

____

____

Draw a picture of your character.

How to use settings

The setting of a story is **where** a story takes place, for example:

- in a castle
- on the beach
- underground
- at the North Pole

The setting can also tell you **when** the story happens, for example:

- long ago in the past
- right now in the present
- far into the future

Read this story and look at the notes about the setting.

David and the Giant

Hundreds of years ago there was a boy called David. He looked after his father's sheep out on the hills in Israel. All day long he watched the sheep and played with his slingshot. One of the king's enemies was a huge man called Goliath. He was ten feet tall! No one was brave enough to fight him, except David.

Where	**When**
in the hills	hundreds of years ago
in Israel	in the past

Setting

What are the settings of these stories?
The first one has been done for you.

The spaceship landed on Mars and the aliens jumped out. They had been to Earth to get food. The aliens had become good friends with the humans on Earth.

Where? Mars

space

When? some time in the future

Long, long ago in an ancient forest, some fairies were flying in and out of the flowers. They were casting spells to make the plants grow. Suddenly, they saw a little girl running towards them – they had to hide!

Where?

When?

It was six o'clock on an early Sunday morning. Jake was in the paper shop filling his bag. He had a lot of houses to deliver to that morning.

Where?

When?

Setting

Writers usually talk about the setting at the **beginning** of a story. This way the reader can clearly imagine what is happening in the story.

Write a story about your favourite day out.
Before you start the story, make some notes about **when** and **where** the day took place.

When	Where

Use these notes to begin your story below.

My favourite day

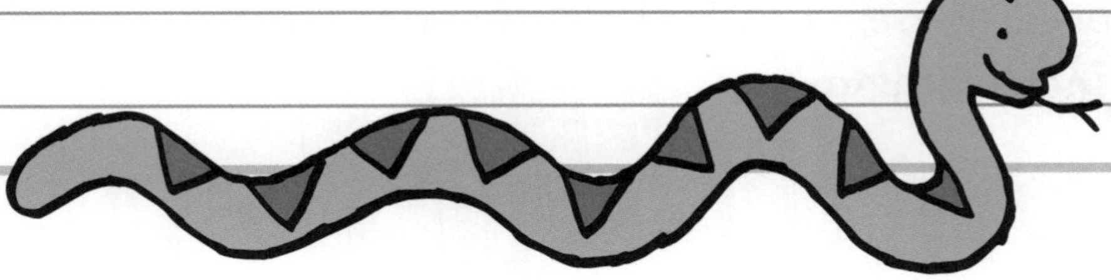

Setting

Now continue your story here.

Remember to include lots of details about the people (characters) in your story.

How to structure stories

All stories need a good structure.

Structure means having a clear **beginning**, **middle** and **ending**.

If any part of a story was missing the reader wouldn't understand what was going on!

Example:

<u>The Ugly Duckling</u>

Beginning

A mother duck sat on her nest waiting for her eggs to hatch. She had been waiting a long, long time. Tap, tap tap! All the ducklings popped out of the eggs. But the last duckling was ever so ugly and clumsy-looking.

Middle

All the other animals teased the ugly duckling because he looked different. Feeling very sad, the ugly duckling left the farm. It was winter and he grew cold and hungry.

Ending

But soon spring came and the ugly duckling spread his wings and flew over the lake. When he landed on the water the ugly duckling looked at his reflection. He was no longer an ugly duckling but a beautiful swan!

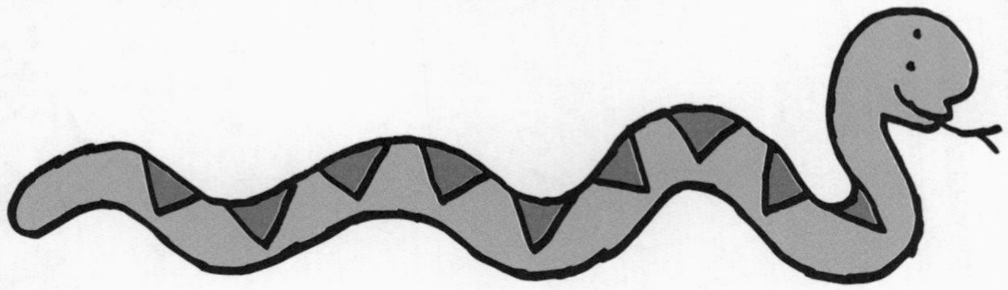

Here is a well-known story. It has been split into a beginning, middle and ending – but someone has jumbled them up!

Try to work out the correct order, then write the letters below.

A Goldilocks saw the open door to the bears' cottage and went in. She tasted their porridge, sat in their chairs and fell asleep in Baby Bear's bed.

B In a cottage in a wood lived three bears – Father Bear, Mother Bear and Baby Bear. Their porridge was too hot so they went for a walk while it cooled down.

C When the bears returned they could tell someone had been in their cottage. Upstairs, they found Goldilocks asleep in Baby Bear's bed! But the bears weren't angry and invited Goldilocks for breakfast.

Order of story

Beginning ________________

Middle ________________

Ending ________________

Structure

The beginning, middle and ending of a story should follow a pattern.

Beginning	Tells you about the setting and the characters.
Middle	Tells you what happens to the characters. A problem usually develops.
Ending	Tells you what happens in the end. The problem is solved!

Think of a story you know very well.

Can you split the story into these parts?

Title ______________________

Beginning ______________________

____

____

Middle ______________________

____

____

Ending ______________________

____

____

Structure

Now it's time for you to be a writer.

Write a story about a day at school when something unusual happened.

Plan your story here with notes about the beginning, middle and ending. Also write some notes about the characters who will appear.

Title ______________________________

Beginning ______________________________

____

____

____

Middle ______________________________

____

____

____

Ending ______________________________

____

____

____

Story

Now you have planned your story, use the notes to write it out here.

Enjoy yourself – you're the writer, after all!

When you have finished your story, show it to your family or even somebody who starred in the story!

How to understand vocabulary

When you write something, the words you choose are very important.
If you use dull words your story will be dull. But if you use exciting words your story will be more interesting.

A **synonym** is a word that has the same or nearly the same meaning as another word.

big is a synonym of **large**
small is a synonym of **little**

Here are some more synonyms.

like	**love**
angry	**cross**
happy	**glad**
start	**begin**
dull	**boring**

Vocabulary

Rewrite this story at the bottom of the page.
For each underlined word think of another word that means the same thing.
Use the words in the box to help you.

One <u>wet</u> morning, Jacob pulled on his <u>wellies</u> and went out to play. At the back of Jacob's house there was a <u>huge</u> garden.

Jacob <u>ran</u> down to the bottom of the garden. He <u>stared</u> at the sky and could tell it was going to rain. So Jacob stood under the <u>ancient</u> oak tree.

Suddenly, it began to rain.

enormous looked old

rainy rushed boots

____

____

____

____

____

____

____

____

How to use descriptive writing

When a writer writes a story or poem they have to describe exactly what they are imagining in their head.

Example:

I have a dog. → Can you tell what the dog looks like?

I have a big brown dog with floppy ears. → Can you tell if the dog is well behaved?

I have a big brown dog with floppy ears who is always getting into trouble! → This is much better!

When you are describing something (a person, place, animal) you should try and think about the following things:

size shape colour movement

age smell dislikes likes

Descriptive writing

Create a strange animal, insect or monster and describe it in as much detail as you can. If you describe it really well, the reader should be able to picture exactly what it is like.

How to write about time

There are special words we can use to describe the **time** in which a story or poem happens.

Here are some simple ones: yesterday
tomorrow

There are some words that can describe a **sequence of events**. This means the order in which things happen.

Example:

When I had finished washing the car, I decided to go for a walk. I walked along the path in the woods and **suddenly** something fell on my head! It was only a twig. **After** my walk I headed back home. **Before** I had put the key in the front door I felt a tap on my shoulder. It was my dad.

Here are some more words and phrases that describe time:

the next minute
an hour later
at that moment
when I had finished
suddenly
after that
before I had started to

Language of time

Choose to write about one of the following items. Describe the order in which things happened using the words and phrases on page 102.

A trip to the seaside	Making a cake	Building a tree-house	Going on a plane	Christmas Day

Story

Now is the time to put everything together.
Use the space below to make notes.
You can choose to write a funny or scary story.

Plan the structure and what the characters are like.
Use lots of interesting language and vary the time words you use.

Story

Now write your story here.

How to understand rhyme

Rhyming words have the same sound at the end.

book	–	cook	Say each pair of words out loud and
pink	–	sink	listen to how they sound.
slug	–	mug	Can you hear how they rhyme?

Read this poem out loud.

<u>Georgie Porgie</u>

Georgie Porgie, pudding and **pie**,
kissed the girls and made them **cry**.
When the boys came out to **play**,
Georgie Porgie ran **away**.

Look at where the rhyming words are.
In a poem the rhyming words come at the **end** of the sentences.
These are the rhyming words:

pie	–	cry
play	–	away

Let's see what happens when we take out the rhyming words and put some new ones in.

Georgie Porgie, pudding and **cake**,
kissed the girls and made them **shake**.
When the boys came out to **run**,
Georgie Porgie was no **fun**.

The rhyming words are:

cake – shake
run – fun

Now it's your turn.
Choose some rhyming words and fit them into the poem.

Humpty Dumpty sat on the ________________.
Humpty Dumpty had a great ________________.

hay	bath	hill
day	laugh	thrill

Circle the rhyming words.

Hey diddle, diddle,
The cat and the fiddle.
The cow jumped over the moon.

I know a funny dog
That thinks that it's a frog.
It loves to jump and jiggle.
This really makes me giggle!

Rhyme

Here is a rhyme you might not have heard before.

Oh, dear me!
My mother caught a flea.
She put it in the teapot,
and made a cup of tea.

Choose from these words to make a new, silly rhyme.

Oh, dear me!
My mother caught a ________________ .
She put it in the teapot,
and made a cup of ________________ .

coffee	bunny	honey
toffee	moose	juice

Here is another rhyme.

Cobbler, cobbler, mend my shoe,
Get it done by half past two.

Choose from these words to make a new rhyme.

Cobbler, cobbler, mend my ________________ ,
Get it done by half past ________________ .

three	four	eight
settee	door	plate

Now it's your turn to be a poet!

Think of some good rhyming words to use before you start to write your poem.

You can use the pictures for inspiration or write a poem about a friend or someone in your family.

How to understand alliteration

Alliteration is a special word used to talk about words with the **same sound** that are close together in a sentence.

Example:

The **sc**ared **sk**unk **sc**urried away.

The letters **sc** and **sk** make the same sounds in this sentence. The letters are different but the sounds are the same and alliteration is all about the sounds in a sentence.

Here are some more sentences with alliteration.

The **sl**ow **sl**ug **sl**ithered and **sl**ipped.

The **gr**een giant **gr**owled and **gr**inned.

The **cr**azy **cr**ab **cr**ossed the road with an ice **cr**eam!

The **fr**iendly **fr**og saved the **fr**eezing toad!

Alliteration

Choose two or three words from the box that start with the same sound.
Put them together to make a sentence.
Your sentence can be silly or sensible!

shampoo twisted black shut shower
two bear odd omelette
orange shuffled bald twinkled
twins oil octopus sheep
blue shark belly

The two twins twisted their bodies.

How to write tongue twisters

Tongue twisters are short rhymes or phrases that have similar sounds in them.

They have a bit of **alliteration** in them but also similar sounds that make the words tricky to say.

Read this tongue twister out loud and listen to the sounds the words make.

She sells seashells on the seashore,
The seashells she sells are seashells I'm sure!

Did you get the tongue twister tied up in knots?

The sounds **s** and **sh** are repeated in the tongue twister.

Because these sounds are very similar they are difficult to say next to each other.

Here is another tongue twister.

Betty better butter Brad's bread.

The sounds **bett**, **butt** and **br** are similar in this tongue twister.

How fast can you say it?

Tongue twisters

Let's see if you can write your own tongue twister.

First decide who it will be about –
a famous person, yourself, or someone in your family.

Next, think of another sound that is similar to the first sound in the person's name.

Example:

The tongue twister will be about Claire.
A sound similar to **cl** is **c**.

Clever Claire can clean cauliflowers!

Your tongue twister will be about ________________.

The sounds you will use are __________ and __________.

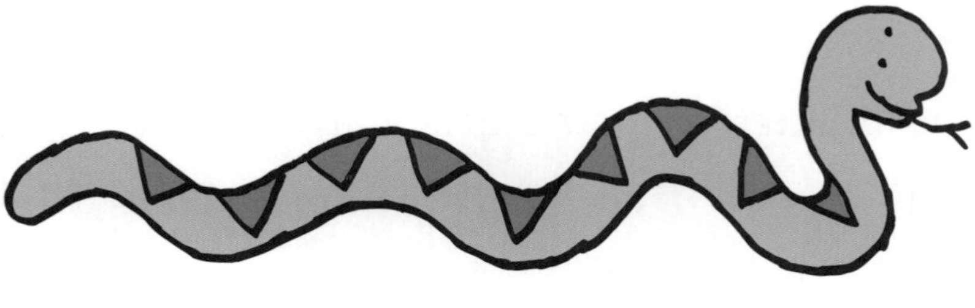

How to write letters

Letters should be written in a certain way.

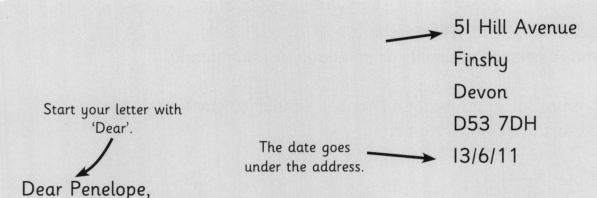

51 Hill Avenue
Finshy
Devon
D53 7DH
13/6/11

Start your letter with 'Dear'.

The date goes under the address.

Dear Penelope,

I'm writing to invite you to a surprise birthday party for our friend Sindy.

It will be on Saturday 16th July at my house.
Please could you arrive at 2pm because Sindy will be coming at about 2:30pm.

Make sure you don't tell Sindy because that will spoil the surprise!

Hope to see you there,
love Saskia.
xxx

If you are writing a letter to a friend your language can be quite chatty.

See you soon! **Take care,** **Bye for now!**

If you are writing a letter to a stranger your language should be polite.

Yours faithfully **Dear Sir/Madam** **Dear Mr/Mrs**

Letters

Now it's your turn to write a letter.
Write a thank-you letter for a present,
or a letter to a child from another country,
telling him or her about yourself.

How to follow instructions

When you write instructions, you need to include **all** the information someone needs to know.

Example:

Instructions on how to make a cake.

If the writer misses out some ingredients or puts things in the wrong order, the reader will not be able to make the cake properly.

When you write instructions:

- put each instruction in the right order
- number each instruction in a list
- make sure each instruction follows on from the instruction before it

Here are instructions of how to get to Alice's school from her house:

1. Walk down the front path.
2. Turn left and walk to the end of the road.
3. Wait at the bus stop.
4. Get on the 370 bus.
5. Get off at the bus stop in front of the park.
6. Turn right and walk to the end of the road.
7. The school is on the left.

Instructions

Write some very clear instructions on **one** of the following:

- how to get from your bedroom to the kitchen
- how to plant some seeds
- how to paint a picture

If you don't write clearly, the person reading the instructions might get lost or go wrong.

How to use labels

Writing labels is a kind of non-fiction writing.
You can write labels for lots of things:

things in your classroom **doors**
pictures and diagrams **maps**

Labels need to be very clear and help the reader understand what they are looking at. Only label things that **need** labelling – don't label **everything** in your classroom, including the floor – that would be silly!

This flower has been labelled.

Understanding labels

How good at labelling are you?
Here is a picture of a human body.
Choose from the labels at the bottom and write them in the correct places.

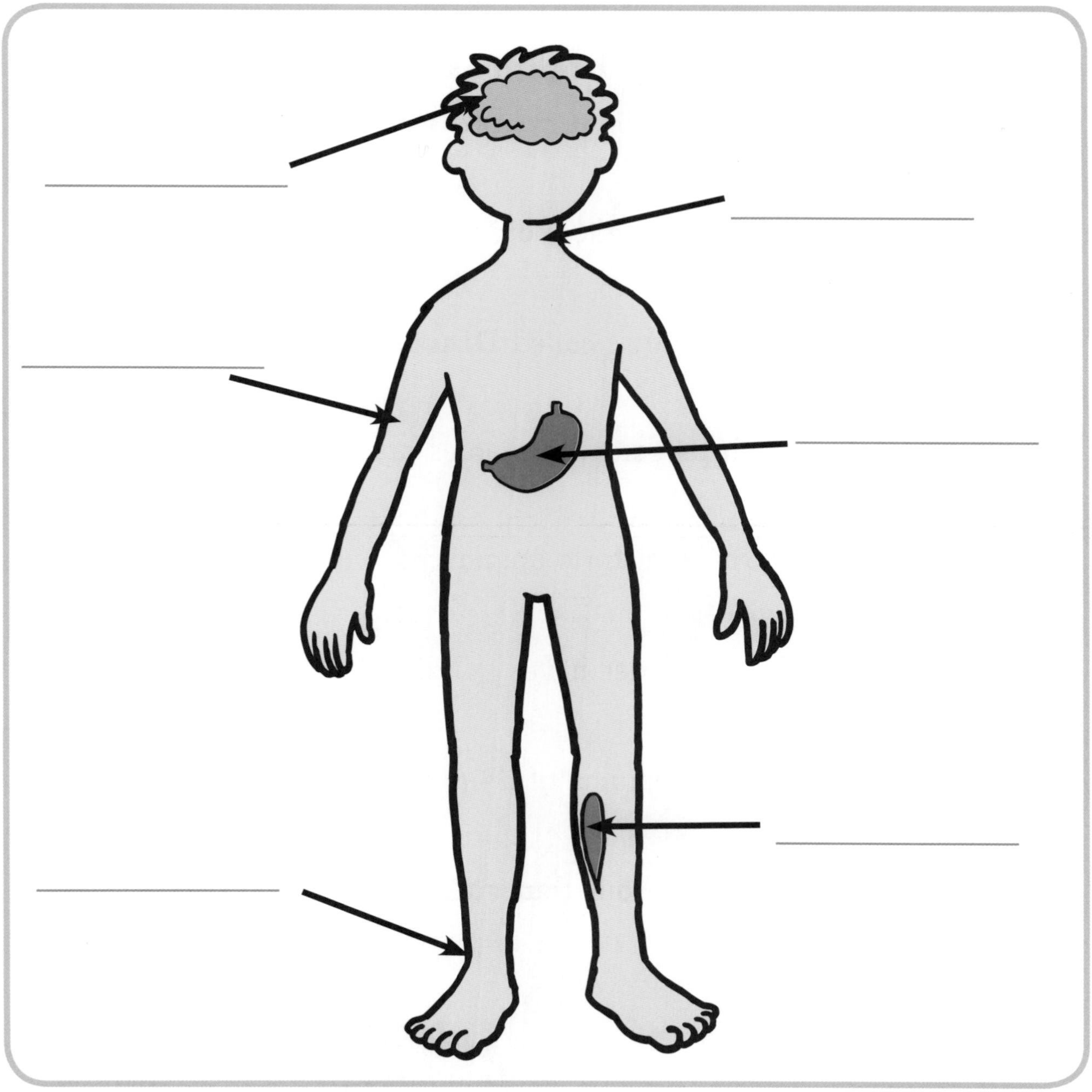

brain calf ankle
arm stomach neck

How to use a glossary

A glossary is a list of words, usually at the back of a book.

It helps the reader to understand some of the words that have been mentioned in the book.

In a glossary there is a list of **definitions**.
A definition explains exactly what a word means.

Glossaries are listed in alphabetical order.

Here is a glossary from a book called **Dinosaurs**.

archaeologist	a person who studies ancient remains.
dinosaur	a prehistoric animal.
extinct	no longer alive.
fossils	the remains of an animal or plant.
stegosaurus	a dinosaur that eats plants.

Understanding a glossary

Write your own glossary for one of the following books:

Computer games
Cars
Animals
Dogs

Think of which words would be useful to have in the glossary.
Which words might the reader not understand?
For each word write a definition.
Look up the words in a dictionary to help you.

How to use fact sheets

A fact sheet is usually one piece of paper giving you lots and lots of information about a topic.

It can have:

- diagrams or pictures
- instructions
- labels
- lists
- puzzles and games
- handy hints
- recipes
- jokes

Here is a fact sheet about exploring the outdoors.

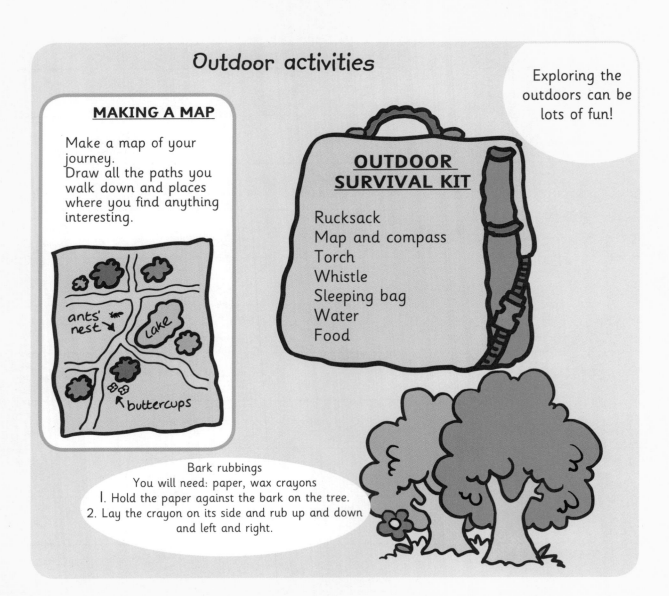

Outdoor activities

Exploring the outdoors can be lots of fun!

MAKING A MAP

Make a map of your journey.
Draw all the paths you walk down and places where you find anything interesting.

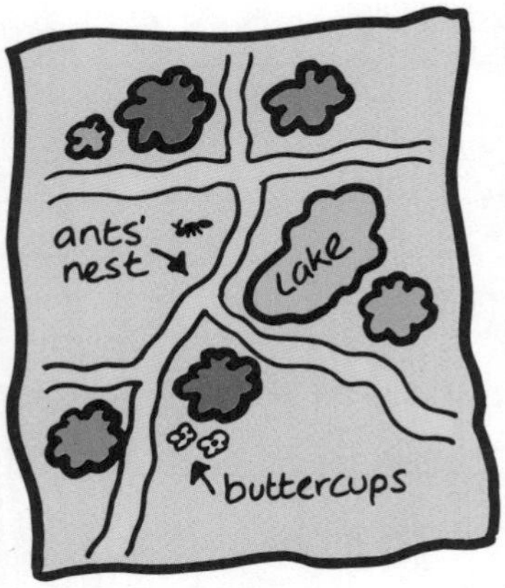

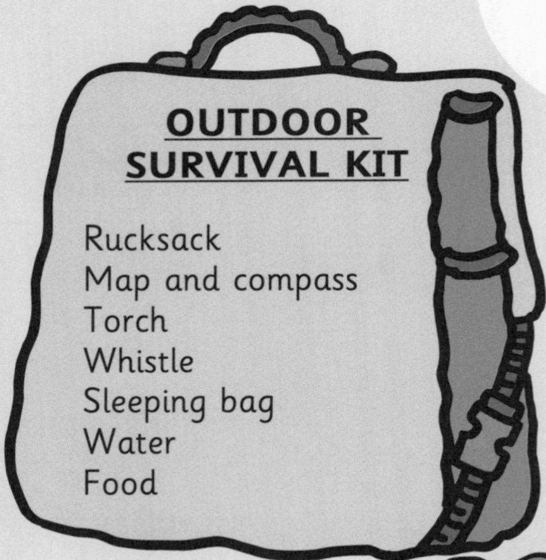

OUTDOOR SURVIVAL KIT

Rucksack
Map and compass
Torch
Whistle
Sleeping bag
Water
Food

Bark rubbings
You will need: paper, wax crayons
1. Hold the paper against the bark on the tree.
2. Lay the crayon on its side and rub up and down and left and right.

Understanding fact sheets

Now it's your turn to write your own fact sheet.
It can be about any topic you like. Write as much information as you can. Here are some ideas: football, hobbies, cooking, TV programmes, film stars, pop singers.

page 87

Accept any story that shows a coherent understanding of character.

page 89

Where	–	in an ancient forest
		in the flowers
When	–	long, long ago
		in the past

Where	–	paper shop
When	–	6 o'clock
		in the morning
		Sunday

page 91

Accept any story that shows a coherent understanding and use of setting.

page 93

B, A, C

page 94

Check that your child has understood how to break a story into beginning, middle and ending.

page 99

wet	–	rainy
wellies	–	boots
huge	–	enormous
ran	–	rushed
stared	–	looked
ancient	–	old

or any other words that show an understanding

page 101

Accept any story that shows a good use of description.

page 103

Accept any story that shows a varied use of time words.

page 107

Accept any rhyming combination.

diddle	–	fiddle
dog	–	frog
jiggle	–	giggle

page 108

Accept any rhyming combination.

page 109

Accept any poem that shows a good understanding of rhyme.

page 111

Check that your child has used alliterative words.

page 115

Check that your child has followed the correct letter layout.

page 117

Accept any instructions that make sense.

page 119

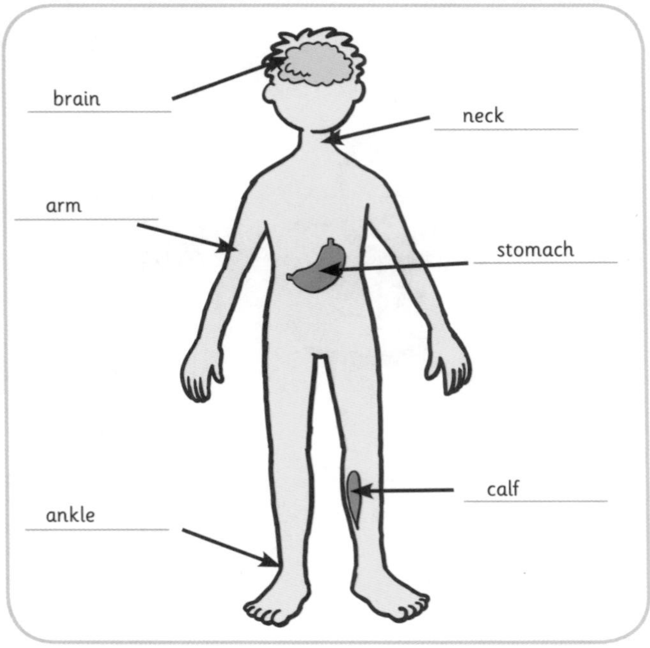

page 121

Accept any clear definitions.

Words you have learnt

character
setting
structure
beginning
middle
ending
vocubulary
synonym
description
sequence
rhyme
inspiration
alliteration
tongue twister

letter
instructions
labels
glossary
definition
alphabetical
information
fact sheet

Checklist

After working through each section, put a tick in the box to show how you feel about the topic.

If you tick 'Not sure' go back to those pages and try again.

	Confident	Not sure
Character		
Setting		
Structure		
Vocabulary		
Description		
Language of time		
Rhyme		
Alliteration		
Tongue twisters		
Letters		
Instructions		
Labels		
Glossary		
Fact sheets		

You can learn with
I Can Learn
The best-selling I Can Learn series is the perfect introduction to learning at home.
Ages 3-4
Count to 10
Get Ready for Maths
I Can Read Letters
Match and Sort
Get Ready for Reading
Get Ready for Writing
Just £3.99
Ages 4-5
Count to 20
Fun with Phonics
I Can Read Words
I Can Write
Learn the Time
Simple Sums
Ages 5-6
Add and Subtract
Maths
Reading
Times Tables
Writing
Spelling
Ages 6-7
Add and Subtract
Handwriting
Maths
Reading
Spelling
Times Tables
Look out for more I Can Learn Megas!
Mega English
Mega English
Mega English
Mega Maths
Mega Maths
Mega Maths
Only £4.99
www.egmont.co.uk/icanlearn